Bearing Hope

BEARING HOPE

Navigating the Desert of Waiting for a Child

by Liv Ryan

Table of Contents

Acknowledgements

Kev: For walking the many miles with me on the dusty desert road, never letting go of my trembling hand. You believe in me every time I fail to believe in myself. You're the cream to my coffee and I love you more than tongue or pen could tell.

Beautiful women of the Bearing Hope Support Group: For month after month, mustering up the courage and energy to "go there." It hurts every time, but you open your hearts and let light into the dark places. As I penned each word in this book, it was your tear-streaked faces I pictured. You've each reminded me to keep my eyes where they need to be, on the giver of life. *This book is for you.*

I pray that as you continue to bravely place one foot in front of the other, you would experience God's love in a tangible way. I also pray for you to have children, as many as your heart and hands can handle.

For my Hope Story Authors: For your stories. For your courage and honesty. For all the hope you're about to bear into the world and the reader of these pages. Thank you.

Lisa: For linking arms with me in the desert of waiting. For bringing me hope, flowers, friendship, and Biblical encouragement when I couldn't stand up. If anyone would have told us on those hot summer runs that in five years we would be raising seven humans between the two of us, we would have laughed so hard! But God has filled our quivers to ridiculously full. Thank you, friend. For everything.

Katie Ganshert: For being an incredible friend and writing Sherpa. Thanks for not letting me give up all 67 times I wanted to! And thanks for the treasures of your books along the way. You have such a gift, and you inspire me like crazy!

Aubs: From becoming wilderness women at Honey Rock, to our late night talks in Smith/Traber, to running the hills of Nashville … for our friendship! Our marathon gave me the courage to take the leap with this book, and you have been an invaluable resource along the way too. Thank you for access to your wealth of Bible and publishing knowledge (and thanks for making sure I don't get any Greek tattoos that don't *quite* make sense.) Come visit with "Grace" and "Handsome" anytime.

Katy: You've walked this journey with me from day one. You taught me what a sisterfriend is and you will forever be one of the best. (Can you please move back to Iowa now?)

Kayleigh, Autumn, Jenny, Lori, Christie, and Melissa: For all the pep talks and prayer this drifting writer needed to cross the finish line. Y'all are ridiculously amazing and it's an honor to do life with you.

Hannah most-talented-artist-ever Slay: For your moving and inspiring illustrations. For your courage through the desert. Thank you! Your work has been such a muse and it's going to bear so much hope. You are brave and lovely.

Rainey: For your psychologist wisdom, beautiful friend! I miss you all the time!

Kev, Mom, Jill, Janet, Karen, Lisa, Jessi, Shannon, my hope story gals, and everyone else who peeked around the manuscript: For your wonderful editing eyes! Thank you doesn't even begin to cover it.

Katie D, Jill, Lauren, Katie G, Paul, Camye, and David: For being my gracious technology Gurus! This book would be sitting in a file on my computer without each one of you!

Leslie, Amy, and the whole Creative Collective: For the coffee, chocolate, and the raddest writing room ever.

For Chris and RosArt: For the beautiful cover art and bearing with me!

"Sometimes, against all logic, against all odds, we still hope."

—Unknown

Introduction

It was a day more perfect than I could have imagined. 80° F was the high, the grass couldn't have been greener, and joy danced in the air. It was July 5th, 2008 and I was about to say "I do" to the love of my life. Dang, he looked *good*.

Looking back, what strikes me the hardest is the innocence and beauty in those moments and in that season of life. The youth ... the desperate longing to "be together" ... the googley eyes ... the future so pregnant with hopes and dreams. I didn't realize it then, but I was wearing an invisibility cloak of naivety.

I am so grateful that on that sunny summer wedding day, I had no idea how much pain the future held for our marriage and family. We had a "perfect plan" as most 21-year old newlyweds do. We wanted to travel and live life jubilantly and freely for two or three years and then start what we saw as the perfect family for us, BEARING CHILDREN! 1-2-3-4-5 ... the more the merrier according to moi!

I would have started trying for kids that very wedding night if Kevin had wanted to, but we were still students and he is more responsible than me. In retrospect, I'm overjoyed that our treacherous journey to parenthood didn't start there. I wasn't ready for the emotional roller coaster that would soon blast us off at full speed.

I'm sure you can relate. Once upon a time you lived in a state of ignorant bliss as it related to having kids.

We watch our wedding video every year on our anniversary (because I'm a sap-ball) and in my personal vows I say, "I will be your biggest cheerleader and best teammate for life, no matter how hard the game may be or how crazy our little teammates are."

When I watch my younger self speak that line through a flirty grin, I want to laugh and cry at the same time because I just had No. Flipping. Idea. I said it, but let's be honest. I didn't know how hard life could and would get.

On that warm afternoon filled with promise and hope, I had not even the slightest inkling that my faith was going to go through a raging battle. I had not one ounce of fear that God might call our "little teammates" home before he called us home. No idea that I would soon struggle so deeply with one of my favorite Bible verses:

> *"And we know that for those who love God all things work together for good, for those who are called according to his purpose."*
>
> (ROMANS 8:28)

Maybe that verse makes you cringe. Maybe it causes your tired heart to ache because you don't feel like there is any way your situation could "work together" to make anything other than the deepest possible pain.

I have been there.

I'm asking you to take my hand and let me guide you through my story, stories of some friends of mine, and some exercises that will help you grieve in a healthy way. We will till up and work through your deepest pain and your heaviest burdens. Together, we will seek to bear joy, strength and hope, even if the darkness of this waiting season persists. I wrote this book for you because you need a companion for your journey. (Preferably a sherpa-slash-friend-type-companion).

* HoPE ! *
(even as your ground underfoot crumbles)

When my life took a turn for the treacherous, I was pretty open about what I was going through. Through sharing my experiences, I realized that so (too) many others had their own painful story but felt alone, hopeless, and discouraged. Out of this season of loss, the Bearing Hope Support Group was birthed.

Once a month a group of women gather around a cup of coffee to share their stories and love on one another. They listen. They pray. They cling to hope for dear life even in the face of infertility, miscarriage, and child loss. The way these women unite, even with such different stories, is breathtaking. They remind each other not to give up, to keep fighting the good fight. These nudges help them put one foot in front of the other, despite all odds. The Bearing Hope Women are the true inspiration behind this book, because no matter how different our stories are, we all need more of the same thing: TRUE HOPE. This companion will help you identify and embrace the source of hope and cling tightly to it through whatever you are facing.

Throughout the book, you will notice comforting verses that the Bible gives us in the midst of our pain. I believe these words pave the path to true hope. If we don't align here, that's okay. But I would encourage you to see the beauty and truth that rises from them anyway.

Not every chapter will apply to everyone, so take the liberty to skip around (in life *and* in the book). There is freedom here! Doodle in the margins. Circle the stuff that dances off the page. Get this book messy! (If you're on your e-reader, don't get too crazy or you'll have to buy a new one.)

The chapters with one-word titles were written with everyone in mind. The ones with more than one word are more specific to certain groups. I think you'll get the hang. The milk and honey sections are like extra credit, if you're the overachiever type.

At the end of each chapter, you will find questions for further discussion. *These are the stuff! You can't skip these, my friend.* Okay, you can, but you shouldn't. More healing happened for me in one conversation with my best friend than eleventy hundred nights crying alone on my floor. I hope to equip and empower you to talk through the hardest-of-hard things. Do you have any friends walking in desert boots too? Consider reading this book together so you can pow wow over Starbys. Your favorite drink here:

_____.

At the teeny tiny least, do some journaling. Capiche?

Your heart will feel happy when you read the "hope stories." Written by women in your shoes, these stories hold waiting, agony, hurt, and more hurt … but their authors still beam hope. Imagine each woman sitting across from you, looking into your eyes, and sharing her heart. These incredibly brave women wrote so that you would realize how "not alone" you actually are.

I'm obsessed with gifts, so I've scattered treasure chests and presents throughout the book. They're all over, waiting to be discovered by your pretty little head. Let's start with these three lovelies:

First, there is grace. Grace meaning: you don't have to have it all together. You can let down your hair and shake it out like crazy. Perfection can be released. You don't have to figure out every day of your future. I know you *want* to but (sorry type A people) – it's impossible!

Second, you are not alone. I'm here (along with millions of other women) and I'm willing to duck down under your sweaty shoulder, hoist you up, and help carry you through this season if you will allow me the pleasure. Why? Because humans were not created to stumble through life alone.

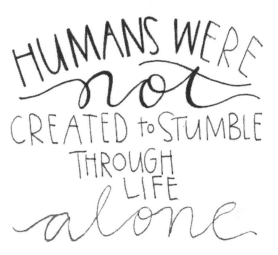

Here's the third piece of ridiculously good news. In the midst of the ugly, black pain and crippling fear … in the middle of your unrealized baby dreams, through your empty womb and empty arms, <u>you can bear hope</u>.

If you can't believe that today, picture me sitting across from you sipping my creamy coffee and saying, "my darling insert name, I believe it for you."

We'll call this waiting you're entrenched in THE DESERT. You're probably parched, trekking through the sand and wind, hoping against hope that you'll get out alive.

You need WATER. And you need it really. Freakin. Bad. The Bible calls it living water.

There is an ocean of hope … a vast sea of grace … a gentle river of peace. Sister, exceedingly-abundantly-better-than-you-could-ask-or-imagine life is waiting for you. I'm so glad you're with me. Put on your scuba gear cuz we're divin' in.

Whoever believes in me, as the Scripture has said, "Out of his heart will flow rivers of living water."

(JOHN 7:38)

"I have been driven many times to my knees by the overwhelming conviction that I had nowhere else to go."

—ABRAHAM LINCOLN

CHAPTER 1

Mine

It was a dark and stormy night. And by night, I mean three years. My life plan was abruptly interrupted on April 14, 2010 when I got the most earth-shattering news I could have imagined. My pregnancy was over. Our baby's perfect little body was right in front of me on the ultrasound screen, but there was no beating heart.

Rewind two months. My innocent young self had woken up to two beautiful lines on a pee stick; now I know how very precious those lines are. I understand how hard it is to wait for those lines and how many women live their entire post-pubescent lives to see them. It didn't cross my mind not to take those exciting moments for granted. I simply thought to myself, "Here we go! The ultimate stage of life is about to begin." And I started onesie shopping immediately.

Fast forward back to that fateful day in April. With the swirling of an ultrasound wand and seven horrible words, "Honey, more people miscarry than you know," I was broken.

I had longed to be a mommy since my baby doll days. But

just like that, in one little moment, it was stripped away.

The doctors scheduled my D&C for two days later. Take my baby? "What if they were wrong about that little heart? What if God brought our baby back to life?" Shock, denial, and fear were the alternating emotions in those first few hours.

That night was the darkest of my life. When we switched the lights off to go to sleep, anxiety crept up and threatened to swallow me whole. In my mind, I was transported back to the ultrasound room and I couldn't stop my emotions from spiraling out of control. I stumbled out of bed and down to the living room. Two hours later (long after sending my sweet husband back to bed), I was still sprawled out on my belly. There were crumpled tissues and a mascara-stained pillow beside my red, swollen face. You know what I'm talking about. I was ugly crying: head pounding, breath blocking, puke-inducing sobs. (We have both fugly cried and that alone makes us sisters.)

Through my bitter tears, I prayed. It was a messy prayer as I laid everything out before God. I didn't hide my fear and anger. "God, what do I do?! Why would you allow this!? Please bring our baby back to life."

I also journaled some of my thoughts and prayers, because writing helps me process. This was part of my journal entry that night:

Thank you God for dying so we don't have to shoulder

the pain of this broken world by ourselves. You know pain better than anyone else. You get it. Thank you for your peace that doesn't make sense. Your word says you draw near to the weary and brokenhearted—to me. If I can have only one thing through this, let it be more of your presence.

Little did I know this would be a prayer I would return to time and time again over the three years that would follow.

What eventually gave me the strength to crawl back into bed that night was the peace of God. That peace didn't make it okay, and it didn't make the pain go away, but it helped me sleep. And inhale. And take steps forward. And none of those things made sense in the face of my anger, longing, confusion, and 11/10 hurt.

That same peace would blanket my fearful heart over and over again. It took us eight months to get pregnant with our second. Month after month, no second line on the pee sticks (and Lord knows I took about 200). Just waiting. And fighting the battle of fear versus faith.

Then came the second miscarriage seven weeks in. **Repeat: devastation.** Enter: fear that something was wrong with me. When we got pregnant a third time, I was a total wreck. *Fear was my life.* Those fears were realized when our third miscarriage placed me in the teensy percentage of women who have three or more miscarriages in a row.

I was infertile, in a strange way. People get that label for a variety of reasons, yours I'm sure different from mine. Mine was through recurrent miscarriage. After tons of tests and vials of blood that had me passing out cold, my recurrent pregnancy loss was deemed unexplained They might as well have stamped BROKEN on my sweaty forehead.

I wanted to give my husband a child, but I couldn't. It was the only thing in my life that I couldn't *work harder* to achieve. I blamed myself and my body because I was the one who was supposed to bear the child.

After lots of prayer and option considering, we started pursuing adoption, since we weren't sure if we would ever be able to have a child the "normal" way.

Fast forward through the months of paperwork, home study, physicals, and seemingly endless other hoops. Hooray! We were deemed "worthy" to join the hundreds of other future parents on the waiting list.

Then, we got the wonderful phone call just two months later. A local birth mom had chosen us! This was not the expected 12-18 month wait we were dreading. We fell in love with the momma and the baby boy she was carrying. I dove into his nursery preparation and we gave him a name, little Carson Samuel.

Our hope grew as her due date drew near. But then came a phone call that falls into the category of phone calls no one ever wants to get. The kind that makes your blood run cold. The kind that leaves you speechless. The kind that you'll never forget where you were when you got it.

It was the social worker. Our beautiful birth mama had changed her mind. It was like a dagger to our hurting hearts; it felt like the cruelest of jokes.

"WHY ARE CHILDREN BEING WITHHELD FROM US?!" I kept asking God. (Obviously in the most reverent-hands-folded-in-my-lap-kinda way.)

There were many days filled with physical, emotional and spiritual exhaustion. The optimism I was inclined to most of my life threatened to be stomped out by doubt and fear. I developed anxiety I had never known before. I was short with Kevin and had little direction in my professional life. I'll be real with you. I sometimes "escaped" by daydreaming about moving to another country and starting a *new life.*

Throughout the whole season of loss, God was knocking on my heart – seeking to capture it. I would be lying if I said I always let him in. But without fail, every Sunday morning my husband dragged me to church. Week after week, the worship band played loudly and people sang at the top of their lungs. Week after week, I sat and wept. In that chair every Sunday my soul was softened and became sensitive to the Lord. I knew he was calling me to have faith, *but it was so hard.* I wept out of pain but also because I was moved.

GOD'S PRESENCE WAS REAL WHEN MY NEEDS WERE SO RAW

In those vulnerable moments, he infused hope into me because I was willing to receive it. I believe those moments kept me moving forward. But hopelessness threatened to return.

* * *

Mere days after our first adoption fell through, I got a Facebook message from a girl we used to attend church with. She was hoping we could get together. "Of course!" I responded. Three days later, we were sitting in my living room catching up after two years of not seeing one another.

Then, she dropped the love bomb on me. "Well, actually the reason I wanted to get together today is because I'm almost twenty weeks pregnant, and I was hoping you and Kevin would adopt the baby." I remember that statement clear as a bell; the rest of the conversation is a blur. I know it involved a few tears, a remark about the awe I felt at God's plan, and a definite YES. The second I closed the door behind her, tears of joy washed down my face for the first time in a long time as I called Kevin with the unexpected "expecting" news.

The very next Wednesday morning, I went to the 20-week ultrasound with our amazing birth mama and we learned together that IT WAS A BOY! I had the honor of attending her appointments for the rest of her pregnancy.

My life was forever changed as I held her strong hand and she birthed little 6lb 3oz Coleton Samuel into the world. The details of that day are sweetly etched in my mind forever. When she laid him in my arms, I remember the hot, fresh tears dripping from my face onto this newborn blondie bundle of joy. She had seven days to change her mind.

We held our breaths. But she was strong, steady, and confident in her decision, at least on the outside. She will forever be a hero of ours.

Coleton carries part of his birthmom's name and we have enjoyed a beautiful open adoption since that Valentine's birthday in 2012. Coleton is our miracle boy, and it's so clear that God created him to be our son.

In the four and a half months leading up to his birth, we lost two more babies. The fifth miscarriage happened naturally at 7 weeks gestation. The bleeding began in the hospital bathroom on the morning of Coleton's birthday.

Profoundly bittersweet.

Our hearts experienced a newfound joy that day, but still carried so much pain. We couldn't seem to escape the loss. Was it time to stop trying for bio children? We wavered back and forth. **The waiting was wearing on us and we didn't want to lose any more babies.** But for some miraculous reason, we weren't ready to give up.

My sixth miscarriage was a chemical pregnancy, which some write off as nothing at all. It's sometimes called a blighted ovum, where a fertilized egg implants in the uterus but the resulting embryo either stops developing very early or doesn't form at all. Since I believe life begins at conception, it was another lost life. Another sweet "little" who spent only a few days with us before going to heaven. At that point on our journey I wasn't surprised, but a girl can hope. And this girl did.

Caring for our little boy was life-changing and wonderful, but it was also hard as we were grieving our lost babies and what seemed like a future without biological children.

The RE (Reproductive Endocrinologist) told us, "You have a 66% chance of eventually having a baby," but each passing loss made our infertility seem more permanent. What if I was the one out of three who would *never* carry full term?

* * *

As I picture myself lying in a heap on my living room floor on April 4th, 2010, the night of our first loss, I'll tell you what else I see. I see Jesus. He is lying beside me with his hand on my back. Comforting me. Smoothing my hair. Singing over me ... breathing into my lungs ... breath after breath ... because on my own I was suffocating.

THE LORD YOUR GOD IS IN YOUR MIDST. HE IS A MIGHTY SAVIOR. HE WILL TAKE DELIGHT IN YOU WITH GLADNESS. WITH HIS LOVE, HE WILL CALM ALL YOUR FEARS. HE WILL REJOICE OVER YOU WITH JOYFUL SONGS.

ZEPHANIAH 3:17

I picture Him lifting my head when I stopped crying and placing it on His strong shoulder. Holding me close. I imagine Him helping me lift the phone to my ear to "untell" everyone. Those were the hardest phone calls I have ever made.

I picture Him carrying me into the hospital for the D&C surgery two days later, because I couldn't have made it there on my own strength.

Throughout the struggles that followed, God's presence came with varying degrees of tangibility. But even in the times I couldn't feel it, Kevin and I look back now and see that He was giving us the strength to press on.

You see, deep down under all my pain was a trickle of hope. It was mostly unbeknownst to me, but it was there, steady enough to form a path through the muck and mire in my troubled soul.

It was that tiny river of hope that kept me from giving up on my faith … my husband … having babies … honestly, life itself. Maybe you don't feel that trickle of hope yet. That's okay girl, stay with me.

I was as shocked as you might be to learn that our story wouldn't end with loss. We would have joyfully adopted again, but God's plan for us looked different. Three years later, almost to the day from when we said goodbye to our first baby, we said hello to our first biological child, Annabelle Hope Ryan. And two years later, yet again, my body birthed another healthy baby, Calvin Micah Ryan. All the tears of joy.

Ridiculous beauty from ashes. *Truly, truly, I say to you, you will weep and lament, but the world will rejoice. You will be sorrowful, but your sorrow will turn into joy. (John 16:20)*

These three children filled our arms quicker than we could've dreamed. If you saw us on the street, you would think me one of those fertile myrtle types—three kids under four and a diaper bag the size of Texas in tow. But if you looked beyond our hot mess, you would see a sparkle in my eye. It's a sparkle that comes from looking at those living, breathing babes and thinking, "Wow, what a miracle."

The first flutter of their movement in my womb had me throwing up in excitement, "Could this be real?" Each kick in the ribs was a gracious reminder that the baby was still with me. I took those pregnancies *one* long day at a time. Finally, labor arrived. As crazy as it sounds, I treasured each painful contraction. The pain resonated through my every nerve as I was brought closer to holding my second and third (but really eighth and ninth) littles. The moments Annabelle Hope and Calvin Micah were laid into my arms are indescribable. They were moments I thought I would *never* live to experience. Three children. I still sometimes can't believe it's real life and not just a dream.

Is life perfect now? Heck to the no. Are my hands full? Is my heart full? Resoundingly yes and yes. But hear me, sweet girl: my hope fulfilled didn't come in the form of baby bundles. My hope came from and still comes from the Lord, the Maker of heaven and earth. The Lord who never grows weak or weary, whose understanding is unsearchable (Isaiah 40:28). It was He who poured out just what I needed to get through those dark days, one at a time.

I can't wait to pour back into you the hope I've been entrusted with. Your soul is thirsty, and ooooh that's a good place to be.

Questions for Further Reflection:

1. What parts of my story can you relate to?
2. How do you process hard things? (circle all that apply)

   Journal

   Talk to someone

   Physical activity

   Play or Listen to Music

   I don't really know

   I typically avoid processing hard things

   Other _____
3. What is your current circumstance? Do you have a diagnosis?

"This wasn't what I dreamed my life
would look like."

—EVERY GIRL WHO EVER WALKED THROUGH
THE DESERT OF WAITING

CHAPTER 2

Dreams

The Garden

Imagine an enchanted forest. You close your eyes and breathe in deeply. Immediately you are swept away by the intoxicating scents of fresh flowers and fruit. You hear birds chirping overhead and elephants trumpeting playfully. When you open your eyes, you stagger backwards. The colors are like nothing you've ever seen, as if you were stepping out of a black and white world into a colorful one you never knew existed. The zebras are playing with the lions, just feet away from hundreds of sleeping antelope. The scene leaves you awestruck. As far as your eye can see, plants are blossoming and animals are abiding in harmony. You take in the diversity and inhale the pure air beside a passionately rushing river. You feel no fear. Only joy … peace … contentment.

Splash of cold water If only a garden-of-eden-existence were our reality, right?

I think it was there, waaaay back in the Garden of Eden, that God implanted in his image bearers the desire for children, after all, God told Adam and Eve to "be fruitful and multiply." (Genesis 1:23)

Wanting Babies

Most humans get pretty excited to picture "mini-me's" running around being adorable. Maybe you have known for awhile that a desire for children was tucked away in you. Or you didn't realize it until you *couldn't* have a baby, but now you're aching because that dream feels lost.

Either way, your family isn't growing the way you dreamt it would. **Welcome to the club.**

Are you a goal setter? A list maker? A box checker? For me, it's a big fat yes to all three. I built my life around my plan, and had always seen having babies as a "right." A guarantee, a non-negotiable.

I wanted to:

- Get married young
- Spend 2 years traveling/rocking a social life/working full-time
- Buy a cute, 3 bedroom house (think white picket fence)
- Start trying for kids at 23 and get pregnant right away (Duh! Young, healthy, and fertile, right?!)
- Birth 3 or more kids and then adopt
- Be 100% fulfilled in my role as a stay-at-home-mom (aka SAHM) and raise up perfect children who are:
  - ☑ well-behaved

☑   smart &

☑   love Jesus.

Think sparkly clean house, teased hair, and lipstick. *Hardie har har har.* We all know how that panned out.

When I was little, we're talking two through forever years old, I could daily be found "pregnant" with or "nursing" my baby dolls. I sang to them, rocked them on my own chunky little lap, and cooked for them in my wooden play kitchen. I was their mommy, and they were my babies. I was made for this, I thought.

As my sisters and I grew up, three words came out of my mouth almost every day according to my mom. "Let's play house!" You can imagine which role I wanted.

When I turned eight, my baby brother was born. Extra special bonus blessing! Everyone said he came from my mom, but by the way I acted, I clearly thought he was mine. I carried him, coddled him, and loved him like I had never loved a human before. "Becoming a real mommy" was solidified in the number one spot on my dream list.

our baby dreams are legit & God-given. but our paths to those dreams aren't as smooth as we wish they were.

Of course we all know some women (or girls) to whom motherhood happened by surprise. I hope and pray that by the end of this book you won't be rolling your eyes at (or let'sbehonest, having malicious thoughts about) those women like I used to.

I'm sure you also have friends who planned their ideal timeline and BOOM! Belly, baby, repeat. Their pretty little lives seem to march right along as expected. I also pray that by the end of this book, you won't be nearly as annoyed by these friends as you might be right now. Every single person goes through deserts of some kind in their life; **no one** has a perfect life.

Have you learned the lingo yet?

ttc lingo:

ttc: trying to conceive
cm: cervical mucus
bbt: basal body temperature
hcg: pregnancy hormone
opk: ovulation predictor kit
iui: intrauterine insemination
ivf: invitro fertilization
re: reproductive endocrinologist: fertility specialist
bfp: big fat positive
bfn: big fat negative
2ww: two week wait
dtd: do the deed
af: oh how we hate you, Aunt Flo
el: evaporation line (especially on the blue tests...
  blue dye needs to die)

Maybe loss has been a part of your story too. Have you endured the pain of a miscarriage? Is there a gravestone in the cemetery with your child's name on it? The pain of these experiences is beyond words. They're things we'll never fully understand on this side of heaven. Our hurts run deep and wide.

Perhaps you are pregnant now, fighting fear day in and day out.

Maybe you're just plain terrified to try again.

Maybe your desert season was a long time ago, but it still hurts.

To every single woman reading this book, I am so sorry.

I know it's not fair.

They're all agonizing, every path in this desert. It can feel like your pain will never end. You want to believe it will, or that you will find some kind of on oasis to catch your everloving breath, but you can't see anything good on the horizon.

Have anger, guilt, depression, or fear become your companions? We'll work on dumping those losers in a few pages, but right this hot second, I want you to enjoy a looooonnnnggg deeeeeeeep breath.

Ready? Let's do this together. Breathe in for six seconds…
Hold for three…
Breathe out for six slow seconds.

Repeat said breath as needed

So the Garden of Eden isn't our reality. Instead we live in a broken world, cursed by sin and full of hurt. You know that all too well. But luckily, the story isn't over. *There is hope ...* so let's flipping talk about it, because it sure hides itself well when you're walking through the desert.

Questions for Further Reflection:

1. What did your "dream life" look like?
2. What have been your most heartbreaking moments?
3. What do you imagine will be the best part about being called "mommy?"

Courage doesn't always roar.
Sometimes courage is the quiet
voice at the end of the day saying,
"I will try again tomorrow."

—Mary Anne Radmacher

CHAPTER 3

Loved

Long before he laid down earth's foundations, he had us in mind, had settled on us as the focus of his love, to be made whole and holy by his love. Long, long ago he decided to adopt us into his family through Jesus Christ. What pleasure he took in planning this! He wanted us to enter into the celebration of his lavish gift-giving by the hand of his beloved Son.

(EPHESIANS 1:4-6, THE MESSAGE)

When I was in the desert, I cried a lot. I cried at happy things and sad things. I cried when I listened and when I talked. I definitely cried when people said the wrong things and I also cried when people said the right things. Get the picture?

I quickly learned that Kleenex was a purse essential every Sunday at church because every stinking service ended with these three words: **You. Are. Loved.**

Church could've consisted of those three words alone and I would've sat there weeping in a heap. You would've thought no one had ever told me that before, but that wasn't the case. I was just more desperate for love than ever. God's love and the love of our church family were like salve on a wound.

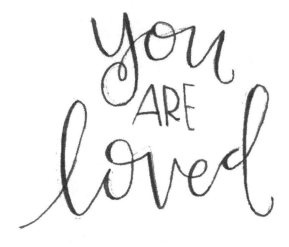

You can't not be touched by that truth. By hearing I was loved, I heard, "God hasn't abandoned you." By hearing "You are loved," I heard "We're here for you, no matter what." And our church family lived it out. They brought us meals. They asked us how we were doing. They loved us like the mighty love ambassadors they were.

If you haven't been loved well by anyone in this season, I'm sorry. That sucks and I'm praying that you find some love warriors really soon. But in the meantime, I'm here and I've slathered these pages with my love. I hope you can feel it seeping into your heart even right now at this very moment. Because you need it.

Knowing I was loved gave me hope. I was loved. I wasn't forgotten. It was rain in the desert.

When we're in hard places, lies love to creep in and whisper, "You're unloveable. You're broken and worthless and undeserving of good things."

But nothing sends those lies running faster than the truth. It's like the way darkness flees when you flood a room with light. Or how the darkest midnight lights up like day with a single bolt of lightning. DARKNESS HAS NOTHING ON LIGHT.

The light shines in the darkness, and the darkness has not overcome it.

(JOHN 1:5)

So I'm about to throw some love injected truth darts your way (like a stealthy pink-ninja-warrior) to obliterate those seedy little lies that have crept in and told you:

"Your husband has had enough."

"You're a mistake."

"You're never going to ever make it out of this desert."

LIE. LIE. LIE.

Ready for your plan of attack back? You look those lies in the face and tell them the truth like a boss:

"I am intrinsically valuable and loved."

"I've been created by and in the image of a majestic God who stretched out the heavens and the earth."

"I have amazing gifts to shine into this world."

"The God of the Universe is on my side."

"This desert season will not define me."

"I. AM. LOVED."

Boom. Drop the mic and walk away.

Questions for Further Discussion:

1. What makes you cry?
2. What lies are you believing?
3. What truths do you need to fill your mind with instead?
4. Practice saying those truths aloud. How did that feel?

Delight yourself in the LORD and he
will give you the desires of
your heart.

—Psalm 37:4

CHAPTER 4

Delight

What does contentment feel like when you're walking in a 200 degree desert with a pack of burdens on your back? Well, I'm not positive. I can't say I walked through the desert with a smile and a skip in my step, but I do want to invite you back into my story. This story is the miracle of God changing my heart's desires.

There are lots of verses in the Bible that make me scratch my head, and Psalm 37:4 is one of them. At first glance, it seemed to imply to me that God is pretty much the-raddest-big-blue genie who can't wait to grant us our deepest desires, whatever they may be. But as I searched deeper, I realized there was more to be uncovered.

First it says, "Delight yourself in the Lord." This scripture verse was urging me to seek my fulfillment in God – in his being, his perfection, his friendship, his love. Well hello, Mr. Easier-Said-Than-Done Bible verse.

But I couldn't let go of this scripture when I was waiting for children. It seemed so promising. It seemed to be saying if I did my part in delighting myself in God, I could get a gaggle of kids. And since that was basically all I cared about in life, or so I thought, I went on a quest to figure out what it meant to delight myself in the Lord. (Although sometimes I was kinda ticked that God was calling me to *do something* when all I wanted to do was stay under my covers all day and drink milkshakes.)

One snail-paced day at a time, I cautiously poked my head out from under my down comforter. I chose to put on my brave girl pants, despite my inevitable stumbling, and do it.

By "it," I mean tried to delight myself in God's love. This included but wasn't limited to: reading my Bible, serving people, praying, attending corporate worship gatherings like church and small group, and singing praises.

Would you guess what happened?

My heart's desires started to <u>shift</u>. *Eversoslowly* but surely they wiggled and jiggled around; it was nuts. I didn't even realize it at the time, but it happened. When I realized that my heart was changing, I felt like it was a miracle, because it was.

Instead of obsessing over the things this world offered like money, recognition, friends, but mostly BABIES (none of which are wrong in and of themselves), I found myself longing to see souls saved, orphans fed, and outcasts embraced. I was much more open to adoption than before, because I could look outside of myself and see, "Oh my goodness, there are tiny people whose parents can't wrap their arms around them and love them well because of their circumstances. Those kids won't have mommies and daddies if other families don't adopt them." And my empty arms felt more purposeful than ever.

I tasted contentment for the first time in a long time. And dang, it tasted good.

And the transformation began. My yearning to grow closer to Christ multiplied as I sought Him. When I grew complacent and discontent, my other longings would rear their heads in a big way. But I kept trekking on like the determined desert warrior I was, and He kept satisfying me with just enough to get through each day.

Mysterious and awesome, God is.

It's almost like he was saying, "Delight yourself in the Lord and he will BE the desire of your heart."

He worked behind the scenes and I worked on delighting myself in him. It was kinda like a walk in the park, except the exact opposite. *I was still in the desert people! And the uphill days were nothing short of excruciating.*

Some days I dragged my feet, which made the journey mucho harder. I remember one specific instance on a Sunday morning. I simply wanted to give up. I waved the white flag and said to Kevin, "I just can't go (to church) today. God feels so far away. I'm lonely. My heart is heavy. I just don't have the energy. You can go without me if you want."

But Kevin wasn't about to let that fly. He isn't legalistic about church attendance by any stretch, but he can spot an excuse a mile away. He responded "I don't really feel like it either babe. But if all I did was try to live in a way that satisfies how I feel in the moment, I would make all sorts of awful decisions (most involving carbs, cheese and sugar). And I would feel terrible. I'm not going to lie, I would *rather* be lazy and snuggle on the couch with you. I would rather drive through the donut place and watch movies all day and feel sorry for ourselves. But we are going to be obedient. Like it or not, we're going to church, girlie. Here's your coat." Or something to that effect.

Busted.

We went to church that morning. And although I remember about 0% of what the sermon was about that morning, I remember walking out of church that day changed. I could pick my feet up again.

Yeah, Kevin is pretty rad. But when I look back at those times, I don't just see a rockin' husband. I see God picking us both up and setting us down facing the right direction again. He sent reinforcements, through whatever means necessary, just in the knick of time, when temptation danced my way.

No temptation has overtaken you that is not common to man. God is faithful, and he will not let you be tempted beyond your ability, but with the temptation he will also provide the way of escape, that you may be able to endure it. (1 Corinthians 10:13)

Whether or not your man is spiritually prodding you, God is using people, places and things to pursue you passionately. He has your ears perked right now, maybe even through the words on this page, and what He has to say to your soul is good.

Girl, don't pull away. Don't let this desert season be a foot-hold for the enemy to keep you away from God and all He has in store for you.

DRAW NEAR TO GOD AND HE WILL DRAW NEAR TO YOU.

JAMES 4:8A

God cares tenderly and deeply. Click play on some worship jams (see Appendix 3). Get your booty to church. Get in your word (find resources in Appendix 2). Find a small group of people who can rally around you. Find your favorite ways to worship and delight in the one who made you so you can draw near to him, and in that nearness, taste contentment. Fulfillment. Satisfaction.

Will seeking God *poof* deliver a baby to your doorstep … or uterus? Probably not. Will seeking him eradicate your desire to bear children? Of course not! After all, he is the one who gave you that desire. But God isn't an old white bearded dude living in the sky, too busy dealing with the world's astronomical problems to hear your prayer for children. And he hasn't forgotten you, though it may feel that way.

He is a tender hearted, personal, perfect, and loving Father with a plan for your life.

As you practice delighting in Him, your timeline may shift. Your patience will grow. Your trust will expand and you'll experience blessings and contentment for your desert trek. Will life be perfect? Heck-to-the-obviously-not.

But it will be water for your thirsty soul.

Questions for Further Discussion:

1. How is your relationship with God?
2. What would it look like for you to delight yourself in Him?

"Don't expect everyone to
understand your journey, especially
if they've never had to walk
your path."

—Unknown

CHAPTER 5

Grace

Raise your hand (or glass) if people have asked you hurtful questions or made comments that make your insides crumple into the fetal position. It may happen as often as *daily*. For the lucky few among us, it's only occasional. These "conversations" are an unpleasant side effect of waiting for a child. They intensify the ache in your tired heart.

- ◆ "When are you guys going to start a family?" (We already *are* a family, see this pretty little ring on my finger?)
- ◆ "How many kids do you guys want?" (umm, well ... one would be nice, to start)
- ◆ "SOOO, when is (Baby <u>last name,</u> baby #2) going to join the party?"
- ◆ "Have you tried _____?" (Not sure I want to go there considering we just met. You don't want to discuss your sex life and medical file with me either? Didn't think so.)
- ◆ "My friend got pregnant after 239204 months of trying.

I'm sure it'll happen for you too!" (Well I hope it doesn't take me 239204 months like it did for your friend. You can't be *sure* it will happen for me.)

- "What's the biggie? At least you already have a child."
- "Whose fault is it?"
- "I guess you just aren't meant to be together because it's not working for you guys."
- "God must not think you'd make very good parents."
- "Just enjoy it and move on with your life."
- "You're young. You have plenty of time."
- "Just adopt!"
- "Trust me, you're lucky you don't have kids!"
- "You just need to relax and you'll get pregnant." (OHHhhhh sister. Or brother. Just…no.)
- "How long have you guys been married now? I thought you wanted to start trying right away."
- "I think _____ wants another little sibling, you really don't want *too* much space between kids."
- "I'm not going to be around forever you know! I will be the best grandparent/aunt/annoying-family-member ever!" "GIMMIE BABIES!!" (Okay, so maybe they don't *say* this but we can read your vibes, bro!)

When people give us unsolicited advice or ask probing questions, here's our three step strategy.

Grace

Humans are not perfect. Amen?! We ALL mess up. We let people down, and sometimes, we just flat out say the wrong things.

One of two things happened when those people said *those things*. Either A, they were oblivious and truly had no idea what you're going through. Or B, they knew and they meant well.

Let's talk about the first one. Once upon a time, you didn't know what you now do. Unless someone close to you filled you in, you had no understanding about the sensitivity involved with what you're going through. Your friends making those comments don't have the same red flags waving in their brains the way you do about certain remarks. There is simply no awareness. Realizing this makes it a little easier to stomach. It makes it a tiny bit easier to dole out what we all need more of: GRACE.

If they do know what you're going through but still said something that made your skin crawl, I want to remind you that they *want* to be loving, helpful and supportive. Your peeps probably don't know what to say so they say what they think is best, which is sometimes quite the wrong thing. They tried, we're going to give them props for not avoiding the conversation altogether. Loved ones would never intentionally heap hurt upon your hurt.

You're hurting, sister. You have to remember that unfortunately you're prone to assume people are being jerks when really your hurt is just triggered by unsuspecting people or things. Sometimes, *nothing* could be the "right thing" for someone to say.

The sting of "wrong things said" or "not said" may never go away completely, but it isn't a reason to be upset with the humans behind the words.

Picture this. One of my best friends had someone say to her loudly in a group setting, "Here's what you have to do. This has a 100% success rate. Just use a turkey baster and … you know …" The lady burst into wild laughter as she nodded her head. Bless.

Though you feel annoyed (and perhaps want to cuss them out), the people behind the poisonous words can't imagine the sting. **These innocent strangers or silly family members, however nosy, inappropriate, or uneducated their comments, need you to give them grace.** If they were in your shoes, they would grimace at themselves too.

Tell it like it is

The second thing that will help us win the battle against the ridonkulous comments is to be honest. People don't want to look like fools, so spare them from being that to someone else. If you don't know them well, you could say a version of "No hard feelings, but that question/comment hurts to hear because we would love to have children right now." Or even "I appreciate the question, but I don't really want to talk about it right now."

The people who know and love you *want to know* what to say and not say. Especially if the situations are recurring. They deserve to know how you feel. Are you comfortable opening up and asking, "Could I share with you what's been going on?" If you're not in a private setting try, "Could we talk about this later?" It will help both of you to have time set aside to discuss what's churning under the surface.

One comment that got under my skin the most was when people found out we were expecting after we adopted Coleton.

"Oh that always happens! I know so many people who got pregnant after adopting!" Objectively speaking, it's not offensive. They simply think adoption ups your chances of having biological children. And they seem so excited!

But I felt like they saw "getting pregnant" as my ultimate goal. Like now I could *really* be happy because we were pregnant and going to have a biological child. Many of them had no idea I had little trouble getting pregnant, but lots of trouble holding a pregnancy. They didn't know how many children I had already lost, or how unsure I felt about whether I would even get to meet the baby I was pregnant with. I felt like that comment belittled our adoption and the love we have for our first son, even if it wasn't intended that way.

Of course not everyone needed to hear the whole story, but people were grateful when we lovingly responded "We've heard that a lot, but honestly it's hard to hear that because getting pregnant isn't our struggle, it's carrying a baby to full term. But we love adoption and what it means, so we would have continued to adopt if that was the plan God had for us! It's crazy how it all works out, isn't it?!"

For some we even let them in on the little secret that that there have been studies done that show pregnancy rates to be the *exact* same among people who haven't adopted and those who have. It just *seems* more common because people are paying attention.

It can be awkward to confront comments that make you want to call your friend a cotton-headed-ninny-muggins. It won't always be easy, but when your experience is honored and heard, it will be worth it. I promise.

If they don't respond gracefully … jump back to numero uno. GRACE.

Grow thick skin

Practically speaking, we have to grow thick skin. The first time my husband's boss gave him constructive criticism, he asked "Do you have your thick skin on?" Weirdo, I thought, after hearing the expression for the first time. But it makes sense now that I've lived a little more. Thick skin is adulthood survival mechanism. It allows you to let hurtful words bounce off and it cushions you to receive criticism well. Maybe you're already rocking a pretty thick skin coat. Go girl!

But if your feelings are fragile, layer up girlfriend. All the girlfriends who have gone before you have had to do it too, or they suffered through being hurt over and over by people who don't mean harm.

You can't control what comes out of other people's mouths, so walking through life constantly offended or afraid of certain interactions is a sucky, stressful way to live. You gotta find that nice big cushiony protective coat of grace and slip it on.

By choosing love and grace, you are choosing peace. You are choosing to destroy stress and fear.

Want to combat the masses in a more proactive way? Write a blog about it and email the link to your friends and family. Or send them a link to some of the ones already out there that express how you feel.

Questions for Further Discussion:

1. Which outrageous comments have you encountered?

2. What do you do when friends, family, and strangers shoot those awful, well-intentioned comments and questions your way? (Cringe? Pretend that didn't *actually* just come out of their mouths? Slap their mouths? Show them grace?)

3. Do a little role playing and practice responding with grace. You got this girl.

"Grieving is as natural as crying when you are hurt, sleeping when you are tired, eating when you are hungry, or sneezing when your nose itches. It's nature's way of healing a broken heart."

—DOUG MANNING

CHAPTER 6

Grief

GRIEVE. I'm not saying it's easy, but I'm saying it's good.

In his book, *Don't Take My Grief Away*, Doug Manning tells of a young couple whose 18-month-old daughter developed a croup and was taken to the hospital. She was put under an oxygen tent and given antibiotics. In spite of everything the doctors did, she died less than an hour later.

When Doug got there, the mother was crying hysterically. He was a young pastor, and he tried to console her. He said, "There, there, you must get hold of yourself." The young woman looked at him straight in the eye and said with fire in her voice, "Don't take my grief away from me. I deserve it, and I'm going to have it."

You deserve to grieve. But did you know that American society is one of only a few without an outward symbol to tell others "I'm grieving"?

In traditional Chinese culture, the 100 days following the death of a family member calls for wearing a colored piece of cloth on their arm. The color of the cloth represents the relationship to the deceased. Families that hold tight to tradition may wear the cloth for nearly three years following the death.

In Russia, Czechoslovakia, Greece, Italy, Mexico, Portugal and Spain people wear black "mourning clothes" after a loved one dies. Widows may even wear black for the rest of their lives.

But here? Oh here in America we're supposed to pull-ourselves-up-by-our-high-heels, right? We're a move on or move out of the way society. Not only does our culture not give much weight to the burden of infertility, but most people assume that we can "just get over it and get on with it."

Oh sweeties. If it were that easy, we would all be skippin' along the rainbow paved roads with scones in hand and butterfly kiss greetings instead of sitting here with this book and Dr. Google and a box of tissues.

You're in a painful season and grief is healthy. It is real. It is good.

Even if we did have an outward symbol for grief, waiting for a child is in an intangible class of its own. Grieving as you wait for a child is so complex—it's up, down, and all over the place. Waiting for a child is extremely difficult to find closure in since you don't know how your story is going to end. Your pain isn't something our society regularly addresses or validates. There aren't many outlets to share your story or what you're going through.

Losing children through miscarriage or stillbirth is talked about more publicly than it used to be, but as the weeks pass, it feels as though the outside world remembers less and less. And it's still a huge source of grief in your life for weeks, months, even years.

When other women _____ (insert your choice of synonym for complain) about "starting" because it's a pain in the butt or (facepalm) complain about "getting their period back after having a baby," you think to yourself, "YOU HAVE NO IDEA."

When you're on this journey, it's always terrible to see blood. Unless of course, you're waiting for that cycle to finally come so you can try all over again. One girl said "it feels like a miscarriage every month."

You are *always* holding on to that sliver of hope that you will be pregnant, or that you won't lose *this* baby. You pray everyday that God will gift you with that miracle baby or lead a birth mom to place her baby in your arms.

You need to grieve your infertility/loss(es).

You *deserve* to grieve your infertility/loss(es).

My uber smart, super adorable Psychologist friend Rainey describes it like this, "If you go about as though your waiting or loss isn't a big deal, but deep down are hurting and suppressing your emotions and grief, it's like putting a bowl full of chicken noodle soup in the back of your refrigerator. That bowl is certainly not going to empty and clean itself. Over time it is going to get stinky. Rancid. Moldy. More harmful by the day."

You may worry if you've been walking through infertility, that grieving intentionally and outwardly means you're accepting that you will *never* have kids. That's not what it means.

Whether or not you get pregnant someday in the future, you are grieving the loss of not having conceived or birthed a child yet.

You're grieving years of parenting lost.

You're grieving the family *that might have been*. And it's healthy.

I wish I had a formula for "grieving your way to peace and fulfillment nirvana." That's a best selling book title if I ever saw one. But wait, the contents of it are BS. We all know life, humanity, and infertility are way too complex for a quick fix like that.

Grieving is not a science, although I'm not sure I'd call it an art either. It can't be reduced to a formula or even a five step process. Grief is unpredictable, individual and complicated. There are probably lots of things you feel that you're embarrassed or afraid to share, but you shouldn't be.

Common Symptoms of Grief

Explosive emotions, like hate, rage, or jealousy: Heightened emotions often take the form of rage, as they are a way to say "I protest this" and to vent your helplessness. The situation you're in does not seem fair.

Relief, release: Since grieving may have been going on a long time, it's very common for grievers to feel guilty about this. Maybe you're ready to release this part of your life and move on, but your spouse isn't and that brings on more guilt or hurt.

Or vice versa.

<u>Feeling trapped</u> by the demands placed on you – pulled from every direction. You feel guilty for not spending enough time with your spouse or family so you increase your time. Then you feel overwhelmed because you don't have enough energy for everyone, and aren't getting enough alone time.

<u>Feeling cheated</u> out of the ability to enjoy "free-time" or hobbies that you once had time for. Or cheated out of the life you hoped to share with the one you lost.

<u>Sadness</u> as you watch helplessly as years of life experiences that you should have had slip away.

<u>Emptiness:</u> feelings of shock, numbness, disbelief, and disconnect

<u>Anger:</u> at God, yourself, or others

<u>Anxiety:</u> panic, fear

<u>Difficulty believing that your waiting will ever have an end</u>

<u>The desire to die or start over</u>

<u>Blaming yourself</u>

<u>Desire for self-punishment</u>

<u>Crying at seemingly random times, for no clear reason</u>

<u>Disorganization, confusion, searching</u>

<u>Inability to perform daily activities</u>

Guess what? It's normal. It's okay.

waiting for a child is scary & hard

You don't need to be embarrassed. Isn't that a relief? If you checked a good handful of boxes, it could be beneficial for you to see a licensed counselor like my friend Rainey. Getting counseling is seeking out healing.

"There is NOTHING weak about being in the care of a counselor. That is STRONG. That tells me that you are not passively waiting for your strength, your healing. You are DOING THE WORK, poking the bear. You are actively working with God and making good use of the gifts He has given someone else to develop us into stronger, healthier people.

Bravo, I say! ...To abuse and suffering and loss and grief and pain and a horrible enemy: I say, COME AT US, BRO. We're not going to take this stuff lying down."

—JEN HATMAKER

A to the MEN. If you're hurting, don't deny yourself the help you deserve. And if you're already getting help—fist pound—you're doing a brave thing.

Counseling can be pricey, but if there were a price tag on emotional health through a dark time, most of us would do everything in our power to afford it.

Kev and I went to counseling through our losses, and it helped more than we expected. Our counselor helped us pinpoint our pain and communicate with each other through it. Our marriage gained some much needed strengthening and the personal benefits were just a bonus. The counselor gave us healthy exercises and conflict management techniques. He helped us step back and digest the fullness of what we were dealing with. He acknowledged our pain. He helped us BREATHE. *Rain in the desert.*

Stages

There are five stages of grief, each with a purpose. Notice they're not numbered? It's because you can't check them off and "move on to the next one." Grief isn't as simple as graduating from point A to point B. You may move back and forth and all around these stages and unfortunately there's no fast forward. You can't rush your grief.

Denial

- You question the reality of your situation or how it will actually impact you
- You have trouble believing or remembering that it's real

Anger and rage

- You find yourself assigning blame
- You want to find someone whose "fault it is"

Bargaining

- You may offer to give up something so you don't encounter the loss, for example, "God, if you give me a child I will read my Bible everyday or quit (<u>fill in the blank</u>)"
- You try to do things that will help you forget

Depression

- You may feel too upset to do anything
- You're very sad, even more sad than you expected.
- You often cry, sleep, or feel incapable of handling life

Assimilation of the loss

- You find yourself better able to deal with your loss
- You're able to give other aspects of your life your time and attention
- Expect this to come in waves, with some days being better than others

Be where you are

If you're angry, this girly book might make you feel like slapping me across the face. I can take it … go ahead … slap my face on the back of the book!

Maybe you're walking with depression and you can't imagine feeling less upset … EVER. You don't want to get out of bed, and you cry a lot. This is common, and it's okay to be here at times. But don't hesitate to reach out for professional help if you think something may not be right.

Try not to force yourself to be somewhere you're not. Swimming against the current is much more difficult than letting it carry you.

I used to worry that I would never exit certain stages. But then, I finally got to leave them for another. Phew! It got harder before it got easier, but the journey did get less treacherous. Relief is coming. *If you can't believe that, I will believe it for you.*

Assimilation

Assimilation means you're able to give energy and care to other aspects of your life. It's basically the best thing since sliced bread for a grieving person. You'll float in and out of this stage, or so the smartie psychologists say, so enjoy the good days when they come! Assimilation is tied to contentment and it's sweet like honey.

You'll have to tell the voices of guilt to leave you alone when things are looking up, because they will try to hold you in your pain forever, those little meanies.

Being here doesn't mean you'll be burden free, but neither will you be when or if you have children. On your good days, there will still be pregnant bellies and cute kids every-freaking-where (especially at Target, the world's coolest superstore, and the place where moms inevitably flock). You will still feel misunderstood or left out at times, but it won't be as crippling.

You also may be closer to sharing your story, even if the ending hasn't yet been written. It is my prayer that someday, no matter where your journey takes you from here, you will advocate for those trudging through the desert—this desert of waiting for a child of which one day you will call yourself a survivor. **You** can connect with them in a way no one else can because **you** have been where they are. Someone way down the road needs you! Your grief isn't in vain, my friend.

I've also racked my brain of a few fun and awesome things you can do while you journey on. This stuff is akin to eating milk and honey in a world where you're used to only dry wafers of bread.

WATCH THE SUN RISE. WATCH IT SET with a picnic dinner. FLY A KITE.
ROAD TRIP LIKE A WARRIOR. BAKE AN APPLE PIE with APPLES You PICKED.
SING KARAOKE. SING IN THE SHOWER. SING IN THE RAIN. SING*SING*SING!
Attend late night movies & shows. TALK HOPES & DREAMS with your spouse
OPEN YOUR DREAM BUSINESS. CONFIDE IN A FRIEND. MAKE COOKIES FROM SCRATCH
WRITE LETTERS TO EVERYONE! GET ANOTHER DEGREE. TRAVEL THE WORLD.
GO CAMPING.   ‖DRINK DEEPLY OF LIFE‖ RIDE A ROLLER COASTER
START A BLOG.   Ride waves. DRAW.
                                                       SCUBA DIVE. PAINT.
"Adopt" a kid or elderly person who needs it. make LOVE. OPEN Your ♡.
Go to the library. Drink coffee in quiet coffee shops. Become an advocate
for the unborn. BREATHE MORE DEEPLY. READ. PRAY. GARDEN. HOPE. . . . .

Mourning

"Perhaps our eyes need to be washed by our tears once in awhile so that we can see life with a clearer view again."

—ALEX TAN

Mourning is the external processing of the pain you feel inside. It's doing tangible things as an outlet for your grief. Do these things as often as you want. They'll provide you relief like a downpour of rain in your driest, thirstiest desert moments.

- Make a Pinterest board that expresses your heart through this journey
- Design or get a tattoo in honor of the children you lost or never had*
- Make ornaments for your Christmas tree for your future children or to represent those you lost
- Write music for your future children
- Write a letter to your husband
- Write a letter to God
- Write a letter to your future child and/or the child you lost
- Paint, draw, or color a picture that represents how you're feeling (hello adult coloring pages!)
- Cry, bawl, yell, and punch your friend named Pillow

- Journal
- Find and attend a support group. Can't find one? Start one!
- Talk to a friend about how you're feeling

* Before you get inked up, you might want to consult your hubby.

Questions for Further Discussion:

1. Who validates your grief?
2. Which stages and characteristics of grief do you find yourself encountering?
3. What have you done to mourn?
4. Which forms of mourning would you like to do more?

Behold, I am doing a new thing; now
it springs forth, do you not
perceive it? I will make a way in
the wilderness and rivers in
the desert.

(ISAIAH 43:19)

CHAPTER 7

Burden

"If you can't fly then run. If you can't run then walk, if you can't walk then crawl, but whatever you do you have to keep moving forward."

—MARTIN LUTHER KING

So you're in the middle of the bleak, barren desert with a mondo burden on your back.

If you had to imagine what your bag of burdens looked like, maybe you picture something like this:

That bag of burdens is SO DANG HEAVY that it almost makes the ground beneath your feet crumble. You can't seem to handle it, but you also don't know how to dump it. No matter how many ways you try to get rid of it on your own, you can't. You can't eat or sleep it away. You can't yoga-it off. It feels UNBEARABLE.

The "waiting for a child" burden can feel so abstract ... so intangible ... so misunderstood. But I want you to try to put actual words on your feelings so you can start to work through them. No matter how heavy your burdens are, it is possible to move forward, and even do so with joy!

To recover joy, though, we need to do something about that big fat burden bag. The first thing is figure out what's in there. I want you to imagine all the STUFF: the emotions, feelings, questions, fears, what-ifs, circumstances, hurtful comments, etc.

Write it all down. Draw your burden bag and write out what you think is in there.

This is what mine looked like like:

Ok GOOD! Maybe your bag is totally stuffed to the brim, even spilling over the sides. Thank you for being real, as ugly as reality can be. It's vital to recognize what's churning in there, causing you so much strain.

Maybe your bag is empty because you have no idea how to put into words what you're feeling. That's okay, too. You can always come back to this exercise.

Now what?

Together we're going to start dumping out, sifting through and processing. You might be tempted to numb yourself, and just skim the words of this book rather than actually do the exercises because, duh, that's easier! It's easier not to *enter into* the hurt. It's easier, we think, to keep it all inside rather than talk about it. That's a defense mechanism I learned well.

But your defenses, though necessary to function at times, can prevent you from processing and moving forward. It is good to dig ... deep deep deep down underneath all that numbness and address the source of the hurt.

Picture your green-thumbed friend pulling weeds from her gorgeous garden. Does she just hack down the weeds on the surface? Of course not, they would shoot right back up! She pulls up the whole root, and sometimes it's deep down in the earth.

Dig deep. Find that stuff and get it down on paper. Then proceed to my favorite chapter.

Questions for Further Discussion:

1. What is in your burden bag?
2. What are your defense and coping mechanisms?

Come to me all you who are weary and burdened, and I will give you rest. Take my yoke upon you and learn from me, for I am gentle and humble in heart, and you will find rest for your souls. For my yoke is easy and my burden is light.

—JESUS (MATTHEW 11:28-30, NIV)

CHAPTER 8

Refuge

Refuge (re-fyooj) *noun:*

1) shelter or protection: a sheltered or protected state safe from something threatening, harmful, or unpleasant

2) sheltering place: a place, or sometimes a person, offering protection or safe shelter from something

The only way to ultimately unload your burden and find freedom and lightness is to hand it off to someone else.

Your doctor doesn't want it. Your husband doesn't know how to handle it. You wouldn't dare give it to your best friend or anyone else for that matter … they would be crushed under the weight. It's too **heavy.**

PSALM 55:22A

CAST YOUR BURDEN ON THE LORD, AND HE WILL SUSTAIN YOU.

You get to heave that ugly thing over your sore shoulders into the hands of someone so able, so strong. The God who created you can handle your burden, the whole blasted thing. And not only can he handle it, but he is *pleading* for you to give it to him. This next exercise is called OASIS.

O•a•sis (ō•āsis/) *noun:*

1)   a fertile spot in a desert where water is found.

Picture yourself trudging along with your fattie knapsack of burdens when you see it appear in the distance. You squint, rub your eyes, and blink a few times. When you realize it's more than a hallucination, your blues (or browns/greens/hazels) get huge and you break into a dead sprint. The closer you get, the louder you hear the babbling brook. Your mouth waters and relief washes over you.

Your shaky legs step from dry sand onto a bridge leading you over a cavern onto an oasis. Lush grass covers a huge clearing, and smack dab in the middle runs a beautiful, sparkling river. You can't tell where the water is coming from, but you don't care. You drop to your tired knees and start slamming handfuls into your mouth. You've never tasted water so refreshing. You wipe away the dripping water from your chin and flop onto your back, your arms outstretched beside you and you sigh loudly. Never before have you felt so safe or relieved. What a magnificent place your oasis is!

This rest is so needed; sister you're exhausted. But coming here required stepping off of the desert road, putting your journey toward a potential resolution on pause. Here you are, resting in the most desperate of ways. Maybe you peek over your sore shoulder and look how far you've come. God has brought you so far. The fact that you're still breathing and putting one foot in front of the other is a miracle.

Sometimes when we stop and meditate on where we are and where we've come from, feelings and emotions erupt from our hearts. I'm a firm believer in letting it all out. Press pause on looking ahead and just feel all of the intense feels deep down in you. Resist the urge to skip this part.

Exercises ala oasis:

1. Find it. If you don't already have a safe haven, a physical oasis where you can be alone with God and your feelings/journal/tears, it's time. Your first challenge is to find your spot and create an atmosphere of refuge. It might be a closet, bed or corner. Maybe it's a private coffee shop or a lovely place outside. Add some pillows or candles, maybe a blanket, a journal and a Bible. Turn on some music, take some deep breaths…settle in.

*Some of you, your battle will be to get here in the first place. For others of you, your struggle is not wanting to leave. These safe spaces are good to go to *for periods of time,* not to stay all the day long. If you are a "feeler" you know that days easily turn into weeks … months … years. Feeling the painful feels can become all-too habitual. Oases are amazing places to process, but they won't teleport you out of the desert. If this is you, set a timer as you move through these exercises.

*   *   *

2. Fill it. Revisit everything that you wrote down in your burden bag. Put them into sentences. Say them outloud. (For example: "I'm exhausted." "I'm so confused." "God how could you let this happen to me?")

* * *

3. Sift. We can get so wrapped up in our burdens that they can start to feel like big ol' fleece blankets. They become our security and identity. Take them away and we feel naked ... exposed ... scared. But freedom starts with being willing to let go.

Remind me of the last time you saw someone running with a big furry blanket tied around her. Oh, never? DUR. Runners don't wear blankets! As you shed your burdens you begin to feel the freedom and lightness to trek on again, even though your pain won't disappear completely.

Imagine yourself rummaging through your burden bag and removing each item one at a time. Look each one over, weighing it in your hands. Think about how it has served you, positively or negatively. If it's not something that will help you in your journey going forward, release it into the river and picture the water washing it downstream. Maybe you pray as you release them. For example, *"God, I give you my anger. Please take it and replace it with joy."*

Use this time to mourn the little ones or time you've lost. Grieve your empty arms. Cry for the years and experiences that could have been. Journal. Write a letter to God, your children/the children you never had, or your husband. Cry, scream into a pillow, or grieve in silence.

Surpass the "functional" layers of padding around your

heart.

Do not be anxious about anything, but in every situation, by prayer and petition, with thanksgiving, present your requests to God. And the peace of God, which transcends all understanding, will guard your hearts and your minds in Christ Jesus. (Philippians 4:6-7, NIV)

As you move through this exercise, you may feel refreshed and lightened. Or you might feel unsteady and emotional.

This trading of your pain and heaviness for God's joy and lightness is a **process**. I wish it was a "one and done" exercise that you could accomplish with a pen and a peppermint latte. But it takes time ... vulnerability ... willingness ... patience. You can come back to it whenever you need to. This is soul therapy ... and bonus, it only costs $0!

Guided Prayer: Lord, I know you are able to comfort me in this deep pain. Please flood my heart with your peace that surpasses human understanding. Take this emotional and physical burden from me. Draw me closer to you. Help me tangibly feel your healing love and hope through this painful surrendering. Steady my feet again the way that only you can. Amen.

Regardless of how the exercise went the first time around, wrap your arms around yourself and take a deep breath. Visualize yourself resting again on the soft grass beside the rushing water. You're exactly where you need to be. You are courageous and beautiful. Each time you do this exercise of visualizing your burdens being released, you lighten your load and make space for some awesome featherweight things like peace, joy, and hope. You're fueling up for the journey ahead.

Proceed to the chapter(s) you feel led to and then meet me back at Chapter 15!

Chapter 9: Permanent Infertility

Chapter 10: It Could Happen

Chapter 11: Secondary Infertility

Chapter 12: Miscarriage, Stillbirth and Infant Loss

Chapter 13: Failed Adoption

Chapter 14: For the Survivor

Questions for Further Discussion

1. Where is your place of refuge?
2. How did the Exercises ala Oasis go for you?

Extra Credit Reading:

Read Isaiah 35 and underline the parts that speak to your heart. Circle the stuff that makes your eyes bug out of your head and say "that's brilliant!" in your best Harry Potter accent. You know how I said you could skip stuff in the book? Well I wouldn't recommend skipping this. These words are rain in the desert, and they're for you today. Right now.

"In the end, everything will be okay. If it's not okay, it's not the end."

—John Lennon

CHAPTER 9

Permanent Infertility

"There is a unique pain that comes from preparing a place in your heart for a child that never comes."

—DAVID PLATT

You will never physically bear a child. The certainty of that reality and the pain that accompanies it are gut-wrenching.

Maybe:

- You have had a hysterectomy or a bilateral oophorectomy.
- You have gone through menopause or premature menopause.
- Your doctor told you that your girly parts are not in working order and your chances are obsolete. Or like my friend Sherry, after seeing your uterus the doc said, "Yeah…you will need to adopt if you want children."
- You've been through failed IVF.
- You've given up.
- You have been told you have a 100% chance of having a

child with a certain genetic disposition so you, your spouse, or together have decided you should be done.

- Your spouse is infertile.

Regardless of how you got here, you are on this terribly difficult road in the desert and you hurt. I am so sorry. No words could make that hole in your heart or that ache in your tummy go away.

Your struggle is not a new one but it *is* a painful one. It *is* a hard one to swallow. The pain of never being able to carry your own child may be a pain that you carry until heaven where pain no longer exists and tears are a thing of the past.

First things first, when you read the hope stories in this chapter, I want you to savor how un-alone you are. These women get it beyond get it. They've left footprints in the same desert sand you're forging your way through.

Next, we're going to talk about your circumstances from a closure standpoint. No matter how far down the "given up" spectrum a woman finds herself when she is in the throes of infertility, the ups and downs of each monthly cycle gives her just enough of a reminder that she shouldn't fully let go. It becomes cyclical pain. Some call it "the crazy cycle." Over and over, month after month, she clings onto remnants of hope for a positive on the test because maybe *this time …* only to be crushed a little more every time her period shows up. There's a good chance you've been through that. You remember.

But you have stepped off of the emotional roller coaster. Sure, you may still constantly be reminded of your inability to get pregnant and that circumstance still threatens to wreck your insides. But as dark as this night looks, you have something many women don't have. You have the gifts of closure and certainty. You can grieve without interruption.

I hope Heather's, Holly's and Leslie's stories lift your spirits today because even though none of them ever gave birth to children, God still turned them into mommies. And my goodness gracious, they bear ridiculous amounts of hope.

Questions for Further Discussion

1. How have you mourned your infertility?
2. When and how did you find out that you would never bear a child (or another child)?
3. How has this journey affected your marriage?

Heather's Story

I always knew I wanted to be a mommy. From the time I was a little girl I dreamed of someday having as many children as possible. I wanted a big family! My mom ran a home daycare and I helped her with the little ones all the time. I always told my parents I was going to give them hundreds of grandkids.

Thomas and I got married when I was twenty four and we decided to start trying for kids just three months after tying the knot. We were giddy excited to get off birth control and grow our family.

We started to fear something might not be right when it had been two years of no birth control and still no baby. I had been late, but never seen a positive pregnancy test. It was then that I went to see a doctor who discovered cysts, which led to a laparoscopy surgery. I was diagnosed with endometriosis but not a lot of guidance was given with what to do with it.

I proceeded to go through a series of treatments after the laparoscopy to prepare my body for pregnancy. After another whole year of no pregnancy, we made the choice to find a new doc as well as embarked on the adoption process.

After a ton of contemplation and a recommendation by the new doctor, we decided to get back on birth control until we were ready to try again.

About a year and a half later, we felt ready. I got off the pill. A whole year passed before I began to get very sick. (It's not what you're thinking). My doc didn't seem to think the pain was related to the endometriosis, but the pain got so bad I couldn't even run a simple errand. Everything I ate made me sick. Working was out of the question.

It turned out the endometriosis was much worse than originally discovered. It wasn't properly diagnosed until nine months and three doctors later. It was the final set of doctors who discovered that my endometriosis had caused a cyst to grow. And not just any cyst. It was the size of a large eggplant. It was pressing against my uterus and obstructing my small intestine. Not only that but we learned that I only had one kidney and the cyst was keeping that kidney from emptying, which was causing the intense back pain I would wake up with in the middle of the night. I couldn't even sleep lying down.

I'll never forget the most heartbreaking day of our journey. We were at the doctor who finally realized the severity of my condition, and he said "I'm going to give you a choice. You can have a hysterectomy when we do surgery to remove the cyst, or you can choose to keep your uterus. Unfortunately, due to the severity of the endometriosis, it's likely the same thing could happen again."

We had questions and the answers were so hard to hear. "The only way to get pregnant if we don't take everything now would be IVF, which would require you to take a lot of hormones that could really stress your ovaries. The pain will be extremely intense."

"What is your opinion?" we hesitantly asked.

He replied gently, "I would have the hysterectomy."

Thomas and I looked at each other and that was the moment. The moment of desperation. The moment the heaviness and pain of it all hit like it never had before. We both knew what we needed to do. Neither of us could stop the tears.

I was 32 years old. "How could this be happening to me? Why would God have given me the desire at such a young age to have babies and then take my ability to have them away from me?" I pleaded for him to make another way.

There was nothing I had done to cause it, but it happened nevertheless. I was the definition of distraught. It carried over into every area of life. I would cry endlessly with what felt like no relief.

At that point, I couldn't wrap my mind around the full extent of our decision and the effect it would have on my life, but I knew it was the right thing to do. Even if it was the most painful decision I've ever made.

The hysterectomy went as well as can be expected. They

took everything: my uterus, fallopian tubes, ovaries, and of course the cyst which ended up being even *larger* than an eggplant. They also took a ton of scar tissue caused by the endometriosis.

From that point on, any hope of us having a biological child was shattered. Devastation hardly covers how I felt inside. The "what ifs" plagued me. What if I had been properly diagnosed earlier? What if we had started trying sooner? What if we had tried IVF?

However, after my initial endometriosis diagnosis, God led us to the foster care system with the intent to adopt. We fostered eleven kids altogether, and one happened to be a newborn baby boy we desperately wanted to adopt. Our hearts were broken yet again when the biological mother chose to have him placed in another home. But then, they arrived. The pair of sisters, ages 1 and 4 at the time, who we fell in love with.

These young girls became our little lights. They called us mommy and daddy and they fit right in with our little family.

We legally adopted them eight months later. Natalie and Emilie are our precious daughters, and if I had to go through the whole mess again knowing that they couldn't be ours any other way, I would do it in a heartbeat.

God used this journey to show me that he is in control of everything in my life. If we hadn't struggled to get pregnant, we would have never begun the process of fostering. And without fostering, we never would have met our daughters. I believe with everything inside of me that those little girls were born to be a part of our family. God had to use another woman's body to make that happen, but I'm okay with that now. Finally.

I will probably never understand why everything happened the way it did in this life, but I am eternally grateful for the opportunity God has given me to be my girls' mom.

I do know that God's plan has always been and continues to be the best plan for my life. What I thought should happen didn't line up with the plans He had for me. But I trust Him because time and time again He has been faithful. I choose (and often have to remind myself) to rest in Him, the one who sees the whole picture. Beginning, middle, and end.

"Fall down, stand up again.
Fall down, stand up again.
Fall down, stand up again."

—UNKNOWN

Holly's Story

I was never able to have children. We tried and tried for more than ten years ... each cycle ending the same awful way as the last. Ten years of hoping and having those hopes dashed. I always had crippling pain with my periods and feared something wasn't right, but I still held out hope for a miracle. The doctor diagnosed me with endometriosis, but encouraged me by saying that I still had a chance of becoming pregnant.

It was a long time ago, so there weren't very many things to try. It was what it was, we thought. No one talked about infertility, but my hurts deepened as the years passed. *It just never happened.*

I was a successful businesswoman, so people made comments about me choosing to live a childless life so I could focus more on my work. That was so incredibly painful and couldn't have been further from the truth. I couldn't believe people would of think me as that selfish.

All in all, though, I count it a blessing from God that he gave me children, even if not from my own womb. The man I married at age thirty had four children from his previous marriage, and I love each one of them as if they were my own. I am so thankful that I had the opportunity to have children, even though they didn't come into my life in the way I imagined they would.

Along the journey, I have had difficult days. I remember days when I couldn't help but mourn the absence of holding an infant who I could have called my own and maybe even seen a little bit of myself in. I've had days when I doubted whether or not my step-kids loved and accepted me as a mother figure. But recently (and keep in mind, I am 67 now and the grandmother of 12) I was brought to tears when I received a letter from one of my kids saying how much I meant to him and how much he loves me. **It's in moments like that when God reminds me he is real and does have a plan.**

> *Jesus replied, "You do not realize now what I am doing, but later you will understand."*
>
> (JOHN 13:7, NIV)

His ways have always seemed mysterious to me, and though it has been cripplingly hard at times, I trust that His plan is better than mine. Things have settled in the childbearing regard, of course. I have accepted my role in life, and I am grateful now for every day that I am given.

I may never understand why things happened the way they

did, but I have realized I am not the one in charge. God is, and I'm just along for the ride of my life.

I look forward to heaven when I believe I'll finally receive answers that make sense and restoration for every longing.

"Even miracles take a little time."

—CINDERELLA'S FAIRY GODMOTHER

Leslie's Story

"What cannot be said will be wept."

—SAPPHO

Kurt and I had planned our family before we were even married. Kurt came from a huge family but he only wanted two kids. I, on the other hand, had always wanted four. Before we even started the journey, we compromised on a plan to have three kids.

We got married and two years later had our first baby, a perfect little girl. Life was wonderful. Then, our world flipped upside down. At just eleven months old, Ann had her first seizure. She was diagnosed with epilepsy and we didn't know the cause.

We were asked by friends and family if we were scared to have another child. Of course we weren't! Although we didn't know the cause of our daughter's epilepsy, we knew there was no history of seizures on either side of our families.

I found myself pregnant once again and loving every minute of it. A little over a year after our daughter's first seizure, our sweet baby boy entered the picture. Wow, what a blessing!

We were still dealing with Ann's seizures but were able to enjoy life as a family of four.

At one point, our daughter's neurologist suggested we do genetic testing to see if that was the cause of her epilepsy. We stuffed that suggestion in our back pocket.

When Ann turned three years old, we learned that she had PCDH19 Epilepsy. It is a condition with a wide spectrum of severity. It causes seizures, cognitive delays and other symptoms, all due to a mutation of the PCDH19 gene on the x chromosome. Males with the mutation, although usually unaffected personally, will pass the mutation onto 100% of their daughters and none of their sons. Women with the mutation have a 50% chance of passing it to their daughters and sons.

This news caused us to pause before going on to try for our third child. There was a chance that our daughter's mutation was "De Novo" or "first," which would present no risk for our future children. But there was also a chance that either my husband or I was the carrier. We made the mutual decision to air on the safe side and get tested. Protocol is to test the father first, so we did.

A gruesome twelve weeks later, my husband got a call from the doctor's office with the results. It was a day I will never forget.

Just two days before our daughter's birthday, I was taking a group exercise class at the local YMCA. As we moved from cardio to core work I checked my phone. There was the text that sent my heart straight into my stomach. The text simply said, "It is me, I have it."

I tried to stay and finish the class but I had to leave because I thought I was going to be physically sick. Our dream of having another child was completely shattered. If we had another girl, she had a 100% chance of having PCHD19. And while our daughter's epilepsy is mild, we have seen how not every case is that way. It wouldn't be fair to that child or our other children. My dreams of carrying another baby inside my body were gone. My hope to have a VBAC and drug free birth were gone. My dreams of cuddling another newborn baby were gone.

I didn't even know how to pray. My heart just hurt.

> *Likewise the Spirit helps us in our weakness. For we do not know what to pray for as we ought, but the Spirit himself intercedes for us with groanings too deep for words.*
>
> (ROMANS 8:26)

I questioned God. "Why is this happening? Am I a bad mom? Do you think I don't need or can't handle another child?"

Every time I got upset with my kids and overreacted, a voice in my head said "This is why—you yell too much. You get mad too often." And other lies just like it.

One Sunday morning in church we sang "Desert Song" by Hillsong. The bridge of the song spoke straight to my heart.

"All of my life,

in every season

you are still God.

I have a reason to sing.

I have a reason to worship."

I wasn't in a great place but I was sure that God was still God and I had a reason to worship! Scripture jumped off the page.

Though the fig tree should not blossom, nor fruit be on the vines, the produce of the olive fail and the fields yield no food, the flock be cut off from the fold and there be no herd in the stalls, yet I will rejoice in the Lord; I will take joy in the God of my salvation.

(HABAKKUK 3:17-18)

My husband and I have nontraditional infertility. We will never bear another child, yet I will rejoice in the Lord. I will take joy in the God of my salvation!

My heart will always long for another child but what an amazing God we serve. I memorized scripture to soothe my hurting heart.

Seek the Kingdom of God above all else, and he will give you everything you need.

(LUKE 12:31, NLT)

He knows just how to comfort us and give us what we need. Just over a year ago our family became a Safe Family (similar to a Foster family) to a three-week-old baby for six months while his mother healed from addiction. Things I never thought I would get to do again I got a chance to do, knowing that it would be my last time. This experience gave me the gift of closure. God has started to comfort me and move me into a place of contentment with our beautiful family of four.

And this same God who takes care of me will supply all your needs from his glorious riches, which have been given to us in Christ Jesus.

(PHILIPPIANS 4:19, NLT)

Praise God for taking care of me, his child. I know that I will be okay.

"There is something incredibly powerful about waiting. It keeps our hearts ready and open. Waiting and wondering are treasures to us when we aren't overly focused on "getting there."

—UNKNOWN

CHAPTER 10

It Could *Happen*

It *could* happen …

Oh I know. The odds are low. Your hopes are low, so that they don't have to get dashed again when you start your period … or when yet another month passes without ovulation.

I'm sure you've imagined thousands of times what it would feel like to see those two beautiful lines on the pee stick instead of the big fat lonely one you always see staring back at you.

One in every eight women between the ages of 20 and 45 in the United States is walking in the same desert at this very moment.

They, too, are desperately hoping they will get to know what a huge baby belly feels like from the inside. They, too, are holding onto a sliver of hope that someday a child will grow safely in their womb.

Even if you have considered other means to become parents, there is still a part of you that wants to feel a baby kick you in the ribs, shop the maternity section, visit the mother/baby unit for *your* birth and experience a child eating from your boobs! Amiright?! For once, you'd like to not feel like the alien in the room when your mommy friends start discussing pregnancy and childbirth.

Maybe it will happen without medical intervention. Or maybe it'll happen with the help of the pharmacist and RE or OB doc. If you end up walking the medical route, I pray that God will help you see the beauty in it. Even if it's not the picturesque way you imagined when you started trying.

As ridiculously long as your stay is in this "waiting room" of life, your heart is tender and pliable for God to shape into something beautiful. We are not going to let the BBT's, cycles and procedures steal your joy—at least if I have anything to do with it.

You're going to have to learn how to let yourself be sad, because hard days are ahead. You also need to allow yourself grace to have good days, because they're coming too! Some days will be tougher than others. But unless God has brought you into a place of peace and rest in pursuing alternatives, don't let go of the hope that some day you will have children.

Trust me, I wandered quite far down the road of "God has obviously made up his mind that I won't have children." But you saw how wrong I was. And you'll see it again in chapter fifteen; God's timing can be quite different from our own.

Deep breaths. Long walks. Lots of hugs. Read on, warrior girl, because it's not time to give up hope.

Questions for Further Discussion:

1. How long have you been waiting?
2. Who in your life understands what you're going through?
3. How is this season affecting your marriage?
4. Where are you in your faith?

"The most fertile place in a woman is not in her womb but in her heart. Because it is in her heart that God births her dreams. It is there in her heart that he plants her desires and gives her the plans for her life. It is where true motherhood begins. Where it lives. And where it grows."

—WAITING FOR BABY BIRD

Emily's Story

I married my high school sweetheart. We were just 16 and 17 years old when we met. From the start, I believe we each knew the other was "the one." We dated for four years and got engaged on Christmas Eve.

We had planned to marry in the Fall following my college graduation. But when we were notified that Jake would be deployed in January, we pulled together our closest family and friends and got married that blustery Midwestern Winter. Twenty sweet days of marriage was all we had together before he headed to Afghanistan.

After spending our first sixteen months of marriage apart, he returned home and we felt ready to bring children into the world. After all, we had been together over ten years! But month after month … no pregnancy.

People told us to relax. They gave us "tips" on things that worked for them. They said some really hurtful things. We weren't stupid, it just wasn't working for us. We were sad, stressed, embarrassed, and upset. Why wasn't this happening easily? We loved each other and were good people. The search for answers began.

Around the holiday season, we found out that we were dealing with male factor infertility. The diagnosis was so grim, we didn't bother looking into fertility issues with my body. We were told it would be nearly impossible for us to get pregnant. We were devastated and at times, angry. We were grieving.

Jake struggled, blaming himself, but I felt that this was not an issue of him or me. We were in this together. It was "us." We wanted a baby together, so we would face this together. I had an odd, peaceful feeling. Something inside of me pushed me to be hopeful and positive. I was drawn to pray.

PRAY. *Sigh* I had been praying since we got a diagnosis. At first, though, I had no idea what to pray for. For an ultimate fix? That this was all a misdiagnosis? For a sense of humor throughout this ordeal?

No ... instead I prayed for strength, peace, and most of all, God's will. If I had learned anything through the years of 9/11, a sixteen month deployment, and a long battle with infertility it was, "My life is not about MY will, it's about God's will."

So, there I was praying for God's will. Something I have NO control over. This should have been a huge struggle for me because I'm a control freak. I have to be the one with both hands on the steering wheel AND changing the radio station. But this time, it was simple. I just said "I give this to you. Take this burden from me and let me do Your will."

This became my prayer. And so I waited, watched, looked for signs.

It didn't take long for God to deliver in a way we didn't expect. Throughout the struggle, people came into our lives, telling us their stories of joy and pain and introducing us to their families. There was one tie that bound all of these families together ... *adoption.*

I didn't think God's answer would come so quickly or easily. I knew that it wasn't MY plan or even OUR plan, but HIS plan. I believed so fervently that adoption was what we were being called to. God was offering adoption to us as a way to grow our family. It hit me that not all children grow inside of a woman's body. Some of them are grown in hearts.

After much prayer and discussion, Jake and I decided that becoming parents to a child was what was important. We agreed that it didn't matter to us how they came to be ours.

We dove headfirst into the world of open adoption. Just six months after being home study approved (which in the adoption world is called "paper pregnant and waiting"), we welcomed our newborn son, Asher, into our lives (along with his birth family!)

Three and a half years later, our newborn daughter, Adeline, joined our family through adoption too. This time we were present at her birth. I cut her umbilical cord and watched her breathe her first breaths.

There are still some days I wonder what it would feel like to have a life stirring inside of me. I dream of whether a child from our DNA would have his hair or my eyes, but that might never be a reality for us. So pregnancy is no longer our ultimate goal.

What IS real is our love for each other, the dream we had to build our family, and the love in our hearts we had to welcome children who were so very, very wanted.

"Storms make trees take
deeper roots."

—DOLLY PARTON

Kimberly's Story

It didn't take me long after going off of birth control, to get pregnant. "Piece of cake!!" I thought. Looking back, I realize how easy it really was.

When I found out I was pregnant I instantly made plans – nursery color, theme, baby name list, registry items, and on and on. My dream was coming true! I going to be a mommy!

Then, my dream turned into a nightmare. I was bleeding and I knew right away that something was terribly wrong.

After my doctor confirmed that I was having a miscarriage (lacking a gentle bedside manner), he sent me to a specialist to better take care of my "situation."

I must admit I didn't handle losing my baby very well. Why would I have been blessed with this precious gift to only have it painfully taken away from me? How could this be a good thing? Or for MY good, for crying out loud? My arms and womb were empty and the darkness was very real. I felt like it was surrounding me all the time.

The loss of a life growing inside of you is devastating beyond words.

So many people told me, "You're young. You have plenty of time." They said, "Maybe something was wrong with the baby and God is sparing you from that difficulty." And then there was my favorite, "Trying is the fun part so enjoy the process of getting pregnant again!"

Ohhhhh my, the things that people say!

Time passed and my husband Chris and I decided that after trying the "natural way" for a year, maybe we should consult a fertility doctor. The wait for this doctor was 9-12 months!

"Why do I have to wait even longer just to be seen? It's going to take forever to have a baby!" my insides screamed.

When we finally got into the specialist, we went through tons of medical questions, a facility tour, and physical exams. My favorite part was her calling us mommy and daddy. She said to get used to the sound of that because soon that's how we'd be known. I had such hope...surely now we will get pregnant!

We met with her again to go over the results of our exams. I was a little nervous but mostly excited. If there WAS a problem she'd be able to help us and our family would be growing in no time. Her conclusion? "There's no medical reason you aren't getting pregnant."

Having it laid out for us was a blessing and a curse. If there's nothing medically wrong, then why wasn't it happening? That brought about more questions. Was this punishment from God for all the things I've done in my past? I knew that wasn't how He worked but I still doubted.

I simply couldn't understand how so many people around us were getting pregnant when we couldn't. I told myself (and others) that some women growing a life inside of them didn't want a baby as badly as we did. It wasn't fair! Each month the pity party for myself grew and grew.

As we started the medical process to have help conceiving, I quickly realized my body would become a human pin cushion. Daily hormone shots, pills, temperature readings, and of course, regular ultrasounds became part of my new normal. When my levels and temperature were right I went in for another implant. The physical toll was intense and painful, but the emotional toll was even worse. The financial toll was quite high as well. Insurance didn't cover any of the doctor visits, procedures, or drugs.

The highs of thinking "this time it will work" and the prayers "God will surely answer this month" kept us at it longer than I would like to remember.

Then there were the lows. The physical pain, the emotional distress, the let down when I didn't get a positive pregnancy test. I felt empty. So very empty.

Each month after a negative result, I needed an ultrasound to make sure there really was no baby. That always revealed cysts on my ovaries, which in turn required birth control for a month to get them down. This, of course, delayed conception and further confused my body by pumping it full of extra hormones.

Not only did this wear on my body, mind, and spirit but it also took a huge toll on my marriage. What was supposed to be joyful and fun became a job. It felt like a scheduled meeting rather than a spontaneous, romantic time as husband and wife.

Having a child became an idol in my life.

I had decided that nothing was more important. Nothing else would make me feel as complete as bringing life into this world and becoming a mommy. This mindset added to the implosion of my marriage.

We had to fix our brokenness and heal. God had a plan for restoration, but it would be a long, painful road.

But in the way only God does, He made us new in Him. He healed our marriage and gave us a renewed view of Him and of what our family "should" be.

It took *years,* but we are finally accepting the call to parent children that didn't come from my womb. God changed my heart from not wanting children unless they came from me to having a strong desire to love and care for children in need.

As I write this my husband and I are blessed beyond our imagination in having an 18-month-old and 5-month-old sibling set in our home. Eight months ago our lives changed drastically for the better.

I never wanted to foster kids. I never wanted to adopt. But now we are doing both and I couldn't imagine my life any other way.

Religion that God our Father accepts as pure and fault-less is this: to look after orphans and widows in their distress...

(JAMES 1:27A, NIV)

I'm learning that true blessing is going where God calls me, being obedient, and leaning on Him for everything, even in the darkness and pain. And I'm seeing what I never thought I would: how He does work everything together for my good and His glory.

I am a momma, not in the way I had dreamed, but in a way that matters so very much to me and to the kiddos placed in my not-so-empty anymore arms.

"It hurts because it matters."

—JOHN GREEN

CHAPTER 11

Secondary Infertility

So you have a child … or children … and JUST when you were done carefully waiting for the right time for another child, you found conception to be so much harder than before. Or maybe you faced infertility the first time around, and were desperately hoping that you wouldn't have to walk this road again. Or maybe you've lost, and you're scared to keep trying. You're scared to get your hopes up, but you want more children. Desperately.

The months tick by ever … so … slowly.

You now know how marvelous it is to be a parent of a living, breathing miracle. You remember what it felt like to have your ribs kicked by your own flesh and blood as he or she grew deep inside of you. You remember the tiny hands ... tiny feet ... the heavenly smell of powdery newborn skin. Your arms ache to cradle another fluffy newborn in your arms and experience the sweet stages all over again. You didn't treasure the other(s) as your last.

The explicit reminders are everywhere. The lonely crib. The calendar reminding you exactly when you have to ... *ya know.* The carefully stacked bins of baby clothes in the storage room. The triggers are different for each of us, but they're all striking.

When your "big" little one grows, you carefully fold each outfit, feeling sad about how fast he/she is growing but imagining how cute the next one will look wearing it ... if there is a next one.

The pregnancy announcements are like daggers to your heart, especially on the bad days. You brace yourself as you log onto social media ... who will it be today? Oh, there it is! Another friend's kid sporting an "Only Child: Expires August 24th" shirt or the cute lined up shoes with a teensy pair interspersed. Your stomach pulls into a knot. You so badly want to be happy for them, but even worse, you want it to be you making that announcement. You try to breathe, calm your stomach, and fight back tears.

Most other moms in your playdate circles and mommy groups have more than one child. Comments have been made, or maybe they're vibing without actually saying things that hurt. Things like, "You have it so easy with just one!" "You wouldn't understand since little Johnny is your only one but my life is so crazy! (But of course it's ridiculously awesome and worth every minute!") You long for the chaos more kids might bring. You long to see yours be a big sibling.

Then there's the guilt. You feel guilty because you already have one or more beautiful child(ren) and it's not that they aren't enough. You are filled with gratitude, but you can't shake the desire for more.

You are not alone.

Questions for Further Discussion:

1. Which explicit reminders have been hard for you?
2. Do you experience guilt because you want to enjoy the child/children you have, but you're plagued with this longing for more?
3. How is your secondary infertility affecting your marriage?
4. How is it affecting your friendships?
5. Is it stealing your joy of parenting the child/children you already have? If yes, how?
6. How has your secondary infertility affected the way you see your little/s now?
7. Has your little one asked you for a little brother or sister? What do you tell him/her/them?

"While it looks like things are out of control, behind the scenes there is a God who hasn't surrendered his authority."

—AW Tozer

Jenny's Story

With the birth of my first child, I "knew" God was fulfilling all my hopes and dreams. I had married the love of my life five years before, and starting a family was just a part of my perfect plan—one that was going well.

Things were easy. Easy birth, healthy, happy baby. Life was good.

When we decided to try for number two, suddenly things weren't so easy. I quit my job as a high school teacher to become a stay-at-home mom. I trusted God. I believed in his promises. But I let my plans and need to control everything drive my relationship with Him and my life. I wanted another baby and I wanted it now.

The timing was good. The situation was perfect, I thought. But ... there was no baby.

There was, however, a whole mess of things I hadn't expected. An emergency appendectomy. Doctors telling me we had to wait months to try for Baby #2. When the time finally came, nothing. No ovulation. No cycles. No baby. Tests were run. Medications were prescribed. I was labeled with "unexplained secondary infertility."

I was put on rounds of fertility medications with ovulation inducing injections. These came along with constant invasive ultrasounds to make sure my "follicles were developing normally" and that I could release an egg.

It was all the opposite of easy and I found myself caught in a tornado of emotions. I was frustrated that my timeline for the "perfect" family was blown up. I was angry that I couldn't control my body and just make it work the way it was supposed to, especially since there was no explanation.

Time passed. I made myself believe that I was feeling pregnancy symptoms. My doctor upped my dosage on the fertility meds. *Horrible side effects followed.* I cried. And cried. And cried.

I got on my face before God. It wasn't the first time I'd done it—literally hurled my heart at his throne—but it was the first time I had done it in a long time. What had been easy my whole life—my Christian walk—was now more difficult than facing the fact that my body wasn't working.

I had accepted Christ as my Savior when I was six years old. I never even considered another path. I was a good girl, raised in a good Christian home. I went to church. I served. I married a godly man. We were raising our son in a Christian home. For me, God had just always been.

As it turns out, I didn't really know him at all. Not like I wanted to—not deeply or intimately or purely. I didn't know this Jesus I had given my life to or what he really wanted from me. I thought he wanted me to be a wife and mom and live happily ever after.

But it seemed like, caught in the storm of uncertainty, he might want something more from and for me. One afternoon while my son was napping, I grabbed my Bible and sat down. I said out loud, "God, I have no idea who you really are. Show me."

Although it was hard for this lifelong Christian to admit that I didn't really know my own Lord, I started a journey that day—a difficult journey of surrender and repentance. And I've never looked back.

In hindsight, I see that if God had allowed me to continue to live such an easy life, I never would have been shaken out of my comfort zone to really seek and know him as my Savior.

Fifteen months passed. I got into the Bible like I never had before. I studied and read and actually enjoyed scripture for the first time in my life. God pushed me into a new passion—writing. He worked in me. He refined me in this season, helping me learn to give up the need to control and replace it with His grace.

Suddenly we were on my last round of fertility meds before we would have to see a specialist and talk IVF—something my husband and I couldn't financially consider. Adoption was most likely out of our financial reach, too. We prayed about it and I got to a place where I could see myself being a mom of just one (a precious, loveable one whom I wanted so badly to see as a big brother).

I went to my doctor's office for the ultrasound and I remember it in stark detail. The tech said none of my follicles had developed well. In fact, one was overly large so there would be no egg—no baby that month. My doctor recommended that we not even do the HcG shot because there was no egg to be released. I mourned what I thought couldn't be. I cried again. So many tears.

It was difficult and painful and I didn't like it. But God was shaping me into someone my husband needed. Someone my son needed. Someone who could minister to other women (although I didn't know it yet) and someone who could use words to touch others. He had altered my carefully planned course of life.

Two weeks later I took a pregnancy test because that's what you do when you're waiting for a child (even when you are sure it will be negative). When that little plus sign appeared, I nearly fainted! I could hardly believe it. I took at least three more. My doctor was surprised, too. Apparently my "overly large" follicle appeared that way because it had already released an egg—all on its own.

Nine months later we welcomed another little boy. My

little man was now a big brother to a tiny boy and my heart overflowed with gratitude. But it was a different kind of gratitude than I'd had after my first son was born. This gratitude was laced with pain and heartache, which made it even more beautiful and special. I knew that this baby boy wasn't a reward for my obedience to God, but a blessing.

Both of my boys were miracles.

A few years later I gave birth to a third son after only one round of fertility medications. We were overwhelmed with gratitude to our Lord but I was tired of what those meds were doing to my body.

We knew we weren't done growing our family—whether through childbirth or adoption—but I just wasn't sure about trying for a biological child again after all we had gone through.

When our third son was two, I saw the same trusty, amazing doctor and he talked to us about the increased risk of ovarian cancer the more I took fertility meds, but sent me home with the prescription in case we decided to try again.

I went to the pharmacy and stood at the counter, shaking; the unease in my heart was overwhelming. I left the pharmacy empty-handed. I prayed. We prayed. I told my husband that I did not want to do any more fertility medications. He agreed. Three precious boys. We were blessed beyond measure.

And then the surprise of baby number four! Even after all

I'd been through, the "easy" of my relationship with God becoming "hard" and then beautiful, I'd fallen back into thinking I could control things. Even after all God had shown me, I thought I was in charge. But without fertility medications, I had become pregnant with baby number four (and yes, it's another BOY!).

It's been a full decade since I carried my first son inside me. A decade of life changes and challenges. A decade of learning what it really means not only to be a mother, but to be a trusting child of God. Looking back on it now, I'm still in awe.

My years of infertility were a struggle but all along God had me in the palm of his hand, and I wouldn't change them for anything. Out of those years were born not only children, but a realization of my own issue with control and a heart eager to seek and serve my God and King. I'm so grateful for the way God stripped my heart bare and filled it up again. I'm sure he's not done yet.

"Sometimes the things we can't
change end up changing us."

—Unknown

Katie's Story

"Faith is the art of holding on to things in spite of your changing moods and circumstances."

—CS LEWIS

Sometimes, things have a way of converging—the stress of a particular situation, fear of the unknown, physical exhaustion, being in an unfamiliar place. All of it gathers together, unearthing emotions that have long been neglected.

I found myself in the midst of this convergence one dark night, in Kinshasa, DRC (the Democratic Republic of Congo) of all places.

Secondary infertility had become a part of my story. For reasons unknown, my husband and I could not get pregnant with a second child. There were sad moments. Worried moments. Frustrated moments. But mostly, I told myself I was okay. We had our son, which was more than most. We should be grateful. And besides, we had always wanted to adopt. So into the adoption pool we jumped, oblivious to the long, exhausting swim we had ahead of us.

I have no doubt, even now, that God has reasons for putting us on this journey. I love our adopted daughter, who is still in the Congo, with every ounce of love in my heart. But I hadn't yet grieved my infertility. And it took going to Congo, spending a glorious, exhausting week with my stranger-of-a-child—this perfect little girl who didn't know me as her mother—to bring that dormant grief to the surface.

It had been a hard day. A she-won't-let-me-put-her-down, I-don't-know-what-you-want, I-haven't-had-time to-eat-anything kind of day. In a foreign, impoverished country where nobody spoke my language. I was concerned about our daughter's speech. I was concerned about her muscle mass, or lack thereof. I was concerned that she seemed so hungry, but had problems eating. We needed to get her home. Start speech therapy. Physical therapy. Food therapy. I was hopelessly overwhelmed. It hit me with so much clarity. Life would never be the same. This adoption road would never get easier.

The grief came and sat on my chest with a weight that felt too heavy.

How was this my life? How had I gotten here—in this broken country with no guarantee of getting my daughter home? I had always pushed ahead. Infertile? No problem, we'll adopt. And in my pushing, I never let myself process the loss. Infertility is loss. **A horrible kind of loss, because what we lose isn't tangible. It's not a miscarriage, where there's life and then that life is gone. It's losing the hope of life, and**

losing hope is a terrible thing.

I grieved all that infertility had taken—the easy road of getting pregnant and giving birth to a child who would know me, and only me, as Mommy. A child unscarred by the injustice of this world. I grieved for my son and all he was missing without a sibling. I grieved all the stress and unknown. And as hard as I tried, I couldn't rally. This grief was the kind that stuck and suffocated.

I crawled into bed beside my daughter, eyes puffy and bloodshot, wondering how I would get up in the morning.

But then the morning came. And you know what? The Lord's mercies were new. Everything wasn't magically all better. The sadness was still there. I had opened the door, after all. I had to let the grief run its course. But I was *okay*. I got up. The sun was out. And when my baby girl woke up, the fear in her eyes upon waking up to an unfamiliar woman in an unfamiliar environment didn't last as long as it had yesterday.

I experienced a dark night of the soul, but God didn't leave me alone in the darkness. He was there with me in it, letting me feel the full weight of my grief. And He was there with me in the morning, taking my hand, telling me to get up and walk out of the darkness. Toward hope.

*Katie now has her beautiful daughter home from the Congo. They've spent the last year bonding and working through more obstacles than she thought possible. Through her daughter, Katie has become well acquainted with the world of special needs and accompanying therapies. While this journey is harder than Katie ever could have imagined, God has been so faithful and so present. He is constantly showing Himself as Provider, Sustainer, and Redeemer.

"Heaven is populated by little souls. If you've lost a baby to miscarriage, complications at birth, an accident, negligence, or even a malicious act of murder, Jesus loves your little one. He has prepared a place for them in heaven. Red, yellow, black or white … born or unborn … they are precious in his sight. They are safe in his arms."

—ROB WILLEY, HARVEST BIBLE CHAPEL

CHAPTER 12

Miscarriage, Stillbirth, and Infant Loss

Oh my sweet girl. Miscarriage, stillbirth, and child loss are some of the most heartbreaking of life's hardships. Babies shouldn't die. And we shouldn't have to say goodbye to our children. It feels so wrong. Unfair. Cruel. Out-of-body. The pain is so fierce.

This chapter has been the hardest to write because there's

just so much. So much to say, yet I am simultaneously at a loss for words.

I'm so sorry. Each baby loss I encountered took my breath away. Every time a friend tells me that she lost her baby, my breath escapes me again. Losses like these just don't make sense in my human mind.

My friend's 18-month-old daughter didn't wake up one morning. Another friend lost all three of her children before they turned five to a terminal genetic condition. A girl in my support group lost eight children in a row through miscarriage. *Jesus, come back and fix this broken Earth.*

These tragedies and losses are nearly painful enough to finish us off. The grief can be unbearable. Does it seem nearly impossible to believe that a good, sovereign God could allow these unspeakable tragedies? Yes, *nearly.*

But it's not impossible. The Bible talks about peace that passes understanding, and Heaven is a piece of that peace. Because we believe our little ones are with God, we can be comforted in knowing that they will never again feel pain. They will never cry tears of sorrow like us. The joy they're experiencing is greater than our minds can even grasp in this moment as your tired eyes dance across the page. To me, that speaks volumes about the goodness of God.

You can rest secure knowing your babies are in heaven. The day we lost our first child, I was desperate to know beyond a shadow of a doubt that the baby was in heaven. My search was officially on. I started listening to sermons, praying, and digging into God's word for answers. What I found dumped peace onto my heart-attack-bound heart.

In the Old Testament, there's a guy named David, you know, the one who killed the giant Goliath with a slingshot and five stones. When he was older, his son fell sick shortly after birth. David begged God to spare the child. He was worried sick. He wouldn't eat or stop praying. He wouldn't listen to "reason" from anyone. Despite his desperate cry for God's help, his son died.

His advisors were terrified of what David would do when he found out. But when they broke the news to him, David got up from the ground, washed himself, put on lotions, and changed his clothes. He went to the Tabernacle and worshiped the Lord. Then he returned to the palace and ate. Everyone was shocked and confused and basically said to him "what the what?!"

> David replied, "I fasted and wept while the child was alive, for I said, 'Perhaps the Lord will be gracious to me and let the child live.' But why should I fast when he is dead? Can I bring him back again? I will go to him one day, but he cannot return to me.
>
> (2 SAMUEL 22:22-23, NLT)

"I will go to him one day" ... did you catch that? David was a man after God's heart. He knew that his eternal destination was heaven, and he said he would go to be with his son someday. When we take our dying breath, we will go to be with our loved little ones. Glory.

I love how in this story David asks, "Who knows whether God will be gracious to me and let the child live?" Because we have no promises about how long any of our littles will live.

This speaks peace to me because I dealt with a ridiculous amount of guilt. **Do you battle guilt? Do you replay the events over and over in your mind and think "if only I had/hadn't _____?"**

Sister, stop. Breathe. That guilt will enslave you. Your baby's death was out of your control. My babies' deaths were out of mine. They couldn't have been prevented with more faith or care. The outcome couldn't have been prevented by us taking more or less medicine, vitamins, bedrest. Even if it seems to be the case.

I *still* find myself occasionally fighting the urge to blame myself, years later. With our first pregnancy, I had extreme cramping on a night I had worked out like crazy at the gym. Two weeks later, we got the news that our baby's heart wasn't beating anymore. The ultrasound revealed our baby to be two weeks smaller in size than expected. I hesitate to even type out that story because I'm terrified of being blamed for my child's death. My tiny first baby who I stared at for hours on the ultrasound picture, willing to come back to life.

But I could either live a miserable life, held hostage by guilt until I meet Jesus face to face or I could walk in the freedom that comes from trusting that it's not my job to give life or take it away. **I believe that God ordains each beat of every single heart. Not me. And that sets me gloriously free.**

YOU HAVE DECIDED THE LENGTH OF OUR LIVES. YOU KNOW HOW MANY MONTHS WE WILL LIVE, AND WE ARE NOT GIVEN A MINUTE LONGER.

JOB 14:5

NLT

Holding yourself responsible is too much to handle, don't you see? A loving God makes those decisions, in his perplexing-to-us-but-perfect-in-eternal-eyes-plan. I hope and pray that the complexity of this will make a heckofalot more sense when we get to heaven.

David wrote in Psalm 23, *"I will dwell in the house of the Lord forever."* He was headed for heaven, where his baby boy lives. And where yours and mine live, too. Can't you almost hear their beautiful little voices ringing?

It's hard to understand how a good, powerful God could

take innocent lives so early. Crystal clear answers don't live here on this broken earth. But I take great comfort in the belief that God has a special place and purpose for their souls.

I believe part of that purpose was shaping me into the woman God wanted me to be. Those babies shaped me into a woman who fights for lives of the unborn. A woman who is sensitive and compassionate to hurting women. A woman who can weep with those who weep and say "I've been there. I've so been there." Their lives were not lived in vain, no matter how short.

Let the little children come to me and do not hinder them because to such belongs the kingdom of heaven.

(MATTHEW 19:14)

When I think about our six in heaven, I'm overcome with gratefulness that they're in a perfect, safe place. But it's bittersweet because I miss them. I want to hold them. Selfishly, I want them here with me. I know you know.

But we can cling to the truth that my lost children and yours are in the unimaginably beautiful place God prepared for them in Heaven. And someday, oh that sweet day that can't come soon enough, we will have the reunion of all reunions.

Healing

Physically, you can't expect yourself to feel normal even though you might look the same. Every loss and each body is different, so be patient. Don't rush the process. Lean in. Feel the feels. *Let yourself grieve.* Find ways to mourn.

Emotionally and spiritually you need to work through the trauma. Sisterfriends, counselors, and hope-filled support groups are great places to start. Find the ones who will weep with you when you're weeping and make you laugh so hard you pee your pants, when you're ready for that kind of joy.

> SISTERFRIEND: (N.)
> A FRIEND WHO IS CLOSER THAN A SISTER. SHE HAS SEEN YOUR GOOD, BAD, AND UGLY AND STILL LOVES YOU. SHE ALSO KNOWS HOW YOU TAKE YOUR COFFEE AND YOUR EVER-CHANGING PANT SIZE

Rejoice with those who rejoice and weep with those who weep.

(ROMANS 12:15)

Remembering your Lost Little Ones

It can be helpful beyond words to have something physical to remember your littles by. Here are some ideas of ways to honor your loves:

8 ways to honor your littles

* RUN A RACE IN THEIR NAME(S)
* MAKE A QUILT WITH HIS OR HER NAME ON IT
* LIGHT A CANDLE IN YOUR HOME ON MEMORABLE DAYS
* GET A PIECE OF JEWELRY WITH THEIR BIRTHSTONE OR SOMETHING SPECIAL THAT REPRESENTS THEM AND WEAR IT CLOSE TO YOUR HEART (I HAVE A NEST NECKLACE FROM MELODYJOY DESIGNS)
* RELEASE A BALLOON ON THEIR BIRTHDAY OR DUE DATE
* START A MEMORIAL, SCHOLARSHIP, OR MINISTRY IN THEIR NAME
* MAKE POTTERY OR AN ORNAMENT WITH THEIR HAND OR FOOT PRINT ON IT.
* KEEP SHARING THE STORY OF THEIR LIFE COURAGEOUSLY

Naming your miscarried children can be another way to honor their memory and help you cope, even if you don't share them with many people or anyone at all.

Don't sweep your feelings under the rug or feel pressured to "move on" before you're ready. Hold onto those physical tokens with fervor. Your child was a *human being*. One that you carried and cared for. Validate that little one's life, however short it may have been. These tiny humans have souls, and they are beautiful.

Guided Prayer:

Lord, thank you that I can hope in you and the promise of heaven. I trust that you can heal and redeem tragic losses. I trust that your plan is bigger than mine. I pray for peace, faith, courage, and strength. I pray that you would carry me when I can't stand. Help me put one foot in front of the other. Redeem this hurt. Heal my body, mind, and heart in a way that only you can. Bring beauty from these ashes.

In Jesus Name,

Amen

Questions For Further Discussion:

1. What is your experience with loss?
2. How comfortable are you sharing about your loss/es?
3. How do you remember and honor your baby/babies?
4. How has loss affected your marriage?
5. Which truths comfort you?

"God can heal a broken heart but he has to have all the broken pieces first."

—UNKNOWN

Mother's Day in Heaven

I imagine the preparations have already begun. They're hanging millions upon billions of beautiful, twinkling lights and setting the grand banquet table.

The blooming trees line the outdoor banquet patio that stretches for miles, clad with flowers of every color and shape and size. The thornless roses are woven together and run up and down the tables, creating the table runners of wedding planners' dreams.

There are giggles and chattering voices galore, as little ones tell each other their favorite things about their mommies. Their little faces light up as they put in their "menu requests" based on their mommy's favorite foods.

They know us so well, better than we even know them! They know our favorite colors, and have already laid out their glimmering robe in myriads of that shade. They'll be slipping them on Mother's Day morning to wear to the feast in our honor.

Our littles! Some of them scamper about the craft room, designing brilliant artwork for the walls in our heavenly house.

Some are stringing together the most breathtaking pieces of jewelry for us to wear some heavenly day.

Their maker watches them with delight ... their perfect little souls worshiping with every movement and thought and hummed melody. Their faces each carefully etched into His mind, as he gently, lovingly reminds our hurting hearts that our littles are more than "just fine." **In fact, they're doing beautifully**. They're not at all worried or hurting or lost, and we needn't be either. We don't need to clutch our memories with tight fists or fear that we'll forget, because we'll be with them soon. And oh, the celebration they have planned for us! *If only we could wrap our minds around it!*

The tiny dancers are rehearsing their brilliant dances. The writers, crafting their poems and stories to recite. The bakers, baking their hearts out. Oh, how the smell of croissants and scones and raspberry macaroons fills the air! The goofballs, of course, are creating plenty of hilariousness for all.

The little musicians are tapping their feet, scribbling their pencils and writing away on their horns ... violins ... pianos. Were we there, their choir of voices would leave us breathless. They're writing brilliant songs that elicit smiles from every parent's face up there, including HIS from the throne. They are so eager and proud to play for us on *that day*.

You know *that day*. **The glorious day on which we're reunited. On** *that day* **we will celebrate** *all* **the Birthdays and**

all the Mother's Days and *all* the painful days in between that we spent apart.

See, the time passes so differently there. They don't feel it in the same slow, drudging way we do. They know *that day* is coming, and it doesn't feel long off to them at all!

They are pumped to finally be swept up, spun around, and then embraced for what will only feel like a second, but will be years. From *that day* on, their Mother's Day celebrations will look a little different. They will get to join their friends who whisper "Happy Mother's Day" into their mommys' perfect ears and twinkle their little eyes at us as we whisper back, "I love you so much."

Our littles who know our wombs so well ... our heartbeats ... our rhythms of life. They will be celebrating us on Mother's Day in a more glorious, breathtaking way than we can imagine.

Happy Mother's Day to every woman with littles in heaven. Soon and very soon, we will get to be with Him and with them, and it will be more than okay.

Courage is knowing that it may not happen, but trying anyway.

—Unknown

Lynn's Story

That time of my life was so dark and stormy it's hard to even go there and recount. I'll have to refer to my journal, because I have blocked out most of the details.

We dated for six years before we were married, so by the time we tied the knot, we were ready to add to the family!

Enter: the years of infertility, miscarriage, and the deepest pain I know to exist.

After a year of trying on our own, we decided to see my OB and we were referred to a fertility clinic to and a half hours away since we lived in a smaller town. We there discovered that not only one of us, but we both had factors contributing to our infertility. I had PCOS (polycystic ovarian syndrome) and he had less than 8% mobility.

They put me on Clomid for 18 months. Still, nothing.

After two and a half years of aching, empty arms and not one positive pregnancy test, we agreed to try IVF. It wasn't going to be cheap, but how do you put a price tag on a baby? We took out a low interest loan … adding financial stress to the pile of emotional and physical stress we were experiencing.

It felt so counter-intuitive, going on birth control to get my cycle more regular for the IVF, but we were at the mercy of the docs who seemed to know a lot more than us. So birth control it would be. I had to drive to a special pharmacy over two hours away.

"It will be so worth it!" I reminded myself.

Enter ... injections. Literally. The wonderful, bruise-inducing-belly injections twice daily for a month. Twenty four eggs were retrieved from my first egg retrieval in that cold, sterile operating room. I remember being in the waiting room with multiple women; it was silent. We were all nervous and hopeful and terrified at the same time.

I left that procedure sore and crampy, but so excited! The chances were good ... we would be having a baby soon!

Six of my eggs fertilized! So after drinking a ridiculous amount of water and taking a Valium, 48 hours (exactly) had passed and the doctor transferred two embryos into my uterus. It was not a pleasant experience, laying on that lab table with my hips elevated. If you want to know the messy truth, I peed on myself from overhydration. They said that wasn't the first time someone had done that, but it was humiliating nonetheless.

Then, enter the longest two weeks of my life. The two week wait with so much on the line. We went out with friends to distract ourselves. We tried to do anything that would take our mind off of "what's going on with the babies?!"

The blood was drawn. The result?! I. WAS. PREGNANT! ME! The girl who had stopped believing it could ever happen. The girl who felt broken. The girl who just wanted to be a mom was finally pregnant!

The first ultrasound was at 6 weeks. I wouldn't have minded twins, but a single beautiful heartbeat made my heart sing! I couldn't WAIT to give my husband the good news, since he couldn't be there. We celebrated and impatiently anticipated the 10 week ultrasound. I could just imagine his smile when he heard baby's heartbeat for the first time.

But he never did. His or her little heart had stopped beating.

We were crushed.

Two agonizing days later I had to have a D&C. Two days after the D&C surgery, we had to take a nine hour road trip to a family wedding. Family wedding meant facing a bunch of people who thought we were pregnant. We had to endure the "I'm so sorrys" and "you'll get pregnant again real soon" comments.

We opted to try again. After our second IVF, we had an early ultrasound and found out this time we were pregnant with twins! It seemed to be too early to find the heartbeats, so we waited. And waited …

We never got to hear those two tiny hearts beating. They

were gone. A month later, after waiting for a natural miscarriage, I underwent another D&C.

On the third round of IVF, my heart just wasn't in it. Our adoption process was in full swing and we were waiting for a call from our agency with a referral. I got a BFP, but again didn't get to hear a heartbeat.

When the adoption agency called just twelve months later, asking if we could consider a local sibling group, we said no. Three children seemed too overwhelming, especially at ages 2, 3 and 4. But after prayer and one night of sleep, we changed our minds.

We brought Rosie, Gigi, and Bubba (as we call them) home just two weeks later! Adjustments followed and insanity often resided in our starter home, but our hearts couldn't have been more full.

Every year on July 30th, we celebrate that very special "Gotcha Day!" Our family came together very much like the fairy tales we read about in story books. Gotcha Day is the day we remember and retell "our story!"

When we share our story with people, I often get the reply "Wow, look what you have done for those kids!"

"No," I respond, "we didn't do anything for them. We didn't save these kids from anything. They saved us. They filled such a longing in our hearts for a family. Their smiles and laughter give us everything we need. And only one person could have known how much we would need each other ... God. He put us together in such a splendid way! It's another one of the many miracles he has performed!"

God destined us for adoption as his children through Jesus Christ according to the good pleasure of His will.

(EPHESIANS 1:5, NRSA)

Six months later I peed on the stick only to find out that I was pregnant ... naturally ... miraculously. Our little Lily girl came to join the fun just fourteen months after we brought our first three children home. We went from a family of two to a family of six in ONE year. Talk about God's plans being bigger than our own!

My home and heart is full, and I wouldn't have it any other way. But that doesn't mean it was easy to trust every step of the way.

"She was brave
and strong
and broken,
all at once."

—Anna Funder

Devon's Story

Text Message

Devon: "Please come home. I need sleep. Drew won't sleep."

Dan: "I'll be right home."

The lack of sleep in the weeks after a child is born is like no other. Unfortunately for my husband and me, that short conversation lead to a tragedy that has forever changed our lives.

On that Saturday night, my husband did what any loving father and husband would do when called upon. He rushed to my bedside as I had been trying to get our two and a half-week-old baby boy to sleep for what seemed like hours. Every time little Drew would drift off into a milk coma, I would set him in his bassinet that was literally connected to our bed. Two seconds later, he would stir. A few seconds later he would begin to fuss.

The only thing I could do to quiet him down was nurse him and hold him close. As soon as Dan entered our room that night, I handed Drew over. Dan closed our door and took him into our living room so that I could get some much needed rest. The next thing I remember is waking up to the most blood curdling scream I had ever heard. As soon as the scream registered in my brain, I knew exactly what had happened. My husband had fallen asleep with Drew and he was dead.

I grabbed my glasses from my nightstand and sprinted down our hall in hopes to prove myself wrong. My husband was leaning over our pale little baby boy, pleading with him to wake up. It was our worst nightmare, but we were very much awake. It was real and surreal at the same time.

The days and weeks after Drew's death are so cloudy. I was anxious, frightened, and continually preoccupied. The questions were relentless: What could I have done differently? Was it my fault? What is going to happen to my marriage? How could I protect my living son? I felt like a zombie, lost in a world so unfamiliar. My worst nightmare had come true and was on repeat in my mind. The fear was overwhelming.

While I wasn't asking God "why," I was definitely living with some big fears and questions. I desperately needed someone to coach me through the next year. I wanted someone to tell me when it would be "okay" to start trying for another baby. I wanted to know how to explain the cemetery to our intuitive two year old. I wanted to know when the extreme feeling of pain would lighten.

In the midst of our darkest days, a friend shared a Bible verse that became my lifeline.

I know what I'm doing. I have it all planned out – plans to take care of you, not to abandon you, plans to give you the future you hope for.

(JEREMIAH 29:11, MSG)

We chose to believe these truths and crawl forward knowing that God had our backs.

Eight weeks after Drew died, I discovered I was pregnant. My husband and I were scared that it was too soon, but we also knew no baby would EVER replace Drew. After a few puzzling questions from our ultrasound technician, we found ourselves in disbelief. We were expecting not one, but two babies! TWINS!

The pregnancy progressed very well. The babies were growing and healthy. On the day of my 36-week ultrasound appointment (almost full term with twins), I hoisted myself up on the table. The ultrasound tech asked about the upcoming 5k race that we were hosting in memory of Drew. As I answered her questions, I quickly noticed her eyes glued to the screen. It was at that moment, I felt my heart in my stomach.

I knew something wasn't right. Within minutes, my doctor was in the dimly lit room delivering the news that "Baby B" had died.

I was speechless. During the entire pregnancy, we kept saying, "God has a plan." But I just couldn't understand how this plan made any sense. How could this be happening again?! Another funeral, another burial?

We were given the options of what would come next, induction or c-section. I wanted to deliver our healthy baby girl as soon as possible, so we opted for the c-section. In my state of mind, I had no idea how a natural labor would pan out.

Within twenty minutes, I was off to labor and delivery to be prepped for a surgery I didn't intend to have.

Because surgery was so unfamiliar to me, I felt the anxiety rising in my body. Several friends had shared their c-section stories in the past and it seemed so easy and routine. But now it was my body they would be cutting open. It was my babies being pulled out.

My biggest fear was how I might react to seeing another lifeless infant. What would it be like hearing one baby announce her arrival while the other had no voice?

But instead of being flooded with anxiety throughout the birth, God gifted me with a sense of peace and bravery. I felt calm and all the worries that had been plaguing me minutes and hours before disappeared. It was a small miracle that meant so much to me. As they rolled me out of surgery, I noticed a room full of friends holding a prayer vigil for us.

Just after 7 p.m., our son Owen William joined his brother Drew in heaven and our daughter Reese Gabrielle arrived bright eyed and healthy.

Our family celebrates Drew and Owen almost every single day. They are both very much a part of our lives and will be until we see them again in heaven.

I have come to accept that comfort doesn't mean the absence of grief. Grief is something we work through; it is a normal, healthy human expression. God doesn't take it away. It comes in waves. God makes our grief bearable. While we see just our little corner of life, God sees the whole. And when we choose to surrender to God in our weakness, we don't have to be strong.

Through our losses, God has given us many gifts and blessings. My kids have a very real understanding of Heaven and embrace it. We are able to give back to parents who have experienced stillbirth or early infant loss through our charity, Drew's Faithful Feet.

While I never would have chosen this path on my own, but because of it, God has refined my family and carried us through our desert season.

"We are all broken, that's how the light gets in."

—ERNEST HEMINGWAY

Kellie's Story

I can't even remember the moment we realized 'infertility' would be such a big part of our lives. But I can tell you that I have dreamed since I was a little girl about being a mommy. College, marriage, children. This was my plan.

Right after we got married, I was ready to have kids. He could wait, but I wore him down! After a year of no baby, we were led to an eventual diagnosis of male factor infertility by the gynecologist and urologist. Our options were IUI and IVF. Being Catholic, we opted against IVF. Plus, the cost was beyond anything we could imagine. We decided to try IUI. First cycle—nothing happened. We were disappointed, but honestly, we weren't sad. It was as though I knew something would eventually work …

On to IUI #2. More medication, ovulation sticks, testing this and that, plus more 'fun'—you know, placing the sample cup in my armpit under my shirt to keep it at body temperature as I drove to the procedure. But this time it worked—we would be having a baby!

We finally had our appointment at 8 weeks and it was

announced that we were having twins. We were blessed beyond our imagination. Both were progressing at the same rate, and honestly the pregnancy was perfect.

Yes, I felt so sick until week 14 and yes, I gained nearly 70 pounds by the end. But there was never any worry, and at 35.5 weeks our baby girls were born, healthy and strong! I didn't realize then how incredibly lucky we were.

More children felt out of the question—twins were both amazing and so hard—but when the girls were about 3 years old, my husband and I felt the same way … we wanted another baby.

Maybe it would happen without intervention. Wouldn't that be cool? I mean, talking about our private life with strangers—even if they were doctors—was not our type of fun. Most of our friends were having baby after baby. Wouldn't it be neat to be able to do the same?

No luck. And goodness knows the effort was made! But life moved on. We had our girls and I landed my dream job as a school administrator. On days when I would get sad about not getting pregnant, I would feel guilty for wanting more. After all, I knew of so many people who couldn't have a single baby, yet here I was with twin girls …

But I wanted another.

I went to retreats and turned to prayer. I heard over and over to "give it to God" and "live God's plan." I tried like crazy to hand it all over to Him, everyday. Everyday I would pray, bless me with another baby if it's your plan"…over and over again.

And then it happened. We had been married for eight years and we finally conceived on our own! Everyone was right! If I gave it to God, it would work!

We were surprised and amazed! It took a full two weeks to get over the shock, and I worried constantly about miscarriage. "Please God, let this baby grow!"

The secret was really tough this time, but we knew we wouldn't tell our girls (who were six) or others until we heard the heartbeat and were well into the "safe" 2nd trimester.

And then I started spotting. I was almost 11 weeks pregnant. We were scheduled to hear the heartbeat the very next day, but the spotting had me anxious.

The ultrasound tech was silent as she searched for a beating heart. I remember after she flipped on the lights and left the room, I looked at my husband and we knew. The doctor confirmed that I would miscarry the child we had miraculously conceived on our own.

The D&C was scheduled for the next morning.

Sadness. <u>Unimaginable sadness.</u>

After the procedure, I was empty. Emotionally and physically.

I loaded up on ibuprofen and after 1 day at home, I headed

back to work. I didn't want to deal with uncomfortable questions so I would just grin and bear it.

I made it through that day and collapsed that night with exhaustion. And then the grieving really set in. I waited until my girls were asleep, but then wailed and screamed into my pillow. My husband sat with me and cried. We eventually fell asleep, but the next day was not any better.

He left to see friends for an annual get-together. I pretended to be strong when he offered to stay home. I said, "we have to move forward" and "I'll be fine."

But I wasn't fine.

That night was the darkest of my life. I truly wanted nothing more than to die. I was so mad at God and I hated myself for buying into this idea of "giving it to God." What had I been thinking? What did it mean to give it to God and then have it taken away? What was God telling me?

The next morning my mom came to get the girls out of the house so I could rest. In that time that I was alone, I grabbed the folder from my last church retreat.

In that folder, I found Bible passages that reminded me of God's love. Many of them made me mad, but reading them reminded me that there would be a time when I would return to God. But I wasn't there yet. I was far from feeling love for God!

I knew I needed to grieve. So I let it happen. I let myself

feel every part of the loss. I tried to spend time with my grief, hoping that the sadness would eventually leave and I would recover.

There was hope. I had people around me to help me get better. I knew healing would eventually happen, although I had no idea when.

It has been two years, and I now know what God was telling me. **It really is His plan. Giving it to God doesn't mean accepting his truth only when you get what you want out of it. Giving it to God means truly handing it over.**

From this loss, my perspective of family life was altered for the better. I quit my "dream job" and discovered that my true dream job was being a full-time mommy. I started to appreciate the small things in everyday life that I had taken for granted—namely the time with my girls. I started to hug tighter and longer. My "I love yous" are passionate and true.

I have forgiven myself for hating God during the loss. And I know that He was waiting for me with open arms, knowing that I would return to Him. I know His love never fails. God was with me through that darkest night...and has been there all along. As much as I tried to scream him away, He kept me in his arms. He loved me the entire time, and I am so thankful that I feel closer to Him now.

*Kellie and Blake have since welcomed another beautiful daughter into their darling family.

"Believe in miracles. I have seen
so many of them come when every
other indication would say that
Hope was lost. Hope is never lost."

—Jeffrey R. Holland

Joanna's Story

Consider it pure joy, my brothers and sisters, whenever you face trials of many kinds, because you know that the testing of your faith produces perseverance. Let perseverance finish its work so that you may be mature and complete, not lacking anything.

(JAMES 1:2-4, NIV)

I have always loved this passage, probably mostly because it contains my favorite word, JOY. Honestly though, up until two years ago, I didn't feel like I had many "trials."

Now I write from a place of having my faith tested far beyond what I could have ever imagined. But I have found endurance and encouragement through the waiting. I know my faith is being perfected, which is a wonderful feeling.

During the summer of 2013, I was finishing my last semester of grad school and was 19 weeks pregnant with our first child. In the midst of a Summer bible study, I desired to deepen my relationship with Christ and prayed to trust Him more.

I never would have imagined what would happen next. I

would certainly have an opportunity to trust God more than I ever had in my life. The rubber was about to meet the road in my faith.

At our 19-week ultrasound we learned that we were having a boy, which was perfect since I had a boy name picked out since high school. We also learned that our son had a diaphragmatic hernia impeding the growth of his lungs which was a very serious medical condition.

In the moment, we chose to trust God like we never had before. We fully believe in God's abundant power and ability to heal. We knew He could touch and heal our son in an instant if that was His will.

We prayed HUGE prayers and had our family, friends, and area churches pray too. We witnessed so many hearts drawn to seek Jesus because of our son.

Josiah David Johnson was born on October 31st, 2013 and was a beautiful baby. We got to spend a glorious month with him at the University of Iowa Hospital. The doctors did all they could to help him. Our Josiah passed away on December 1st, 2013.

We never dreamed of losing a child. There were countless fearful and uncertain moments where I clung to scripture for dear life.

"You keep him in perfect peace whose mind is stayed on you, because he trusts in you."

(ISAIAH 26:3)

The next summer my husband and I found out we were pregnant and started dreaming of our future again. But when we went to the 10 week ultrasound, we found out the baby didn't have a heartbeat. We experienced much sadness through this miscarriage, but found comfort from encouraging friends who had experienced similar losses.

I never thought I would have another miscarriage, but the day after Thanksgiving I had my second. **We had experienced three losses within one year.**

So now, I write to you in the midst of our waiting. I don't know the end to our earthly story, but I do know that we have three beautiful babies in Heaven that we will someday get to spend eternity with.

Recently, I've thought much about the purpose of "waiting" for our family. I don't know all of the reasons for why we are the ones, along with many others, who get to wait even longer to be parents of children here on earth. **I rejoice with my friends, each time they share they are expecting again, but I also feel so much for my other friends who are in the "waiting". My desire for a baby is even greater than what it was two years ago and I so long to be a mom of a baby here on earth.**

I have my moments where the tears are streaming from the sadness of all we've been through. And it comforts me so much when my husband just hugs me and says "I love you" because often there are no other words that help.

I think a lot about how God can be glorified through my life right now. I'm certain that my purpose and identity are not fulfilled in being a mom, but in being a child of Christ and living my life to bring Him glory.

With the time given to us during this waiting, my husband and I have been able to pour into the lives of our small group members and serve them in unique ways. My husband and I can be spontaneous together, like popping into stores on a whim or biking across town. We've also gone on some pretty cool trips to National Parks.

I'm able to teach a college class that I would've never had the time for if I had children to care for. I have the pleasure of attending the *Bearing Hope* miscarriage and infant loss support group that meets each month. I know "pleasure" doesn't seem like the right word, but I so look forward to this meeting each month and have met extraordinary women that are right there beside me in the waiting. We find healing from sharing our stories, encouraging one another, and studying scripture together.

And God's word continues to nourish me daily, especially in the hardest moments.

I remain confident of this: I will see the goodness of the Lord in the land of the living. Wait for the Lord; be strong and take heart. Wait for the Lord.

(PSALM 27:13-14, NIV)

"If the sky falls, hold up
your hands."

—Anonymous

CHAPTER 13

Failed Adoption

Adoption is an adventure of its own kind, isn't it?! Referrals. Birth mommies and daddies. Countries. Laws. Financials. Questions up to your neck. Decisions that make your tummy do gymnastics. Phone calls and interviews and all sorts of unknowns. It can be miraculous when it goes right. But when it goes wrong, your sky can fall.

All that time, energy, prayer … and now *this*. Maybe:

- You lost your referral.

- Your birth mom changed her mind.

- You brought your child home and then was taken away.

- The country you were working with closed or did something unthinkable.

The pain of losing a child is so intense and I'm so sorry.

I can relate. When we went through the home study process, I was giddy. Our desert journey of waiting for a child, I thought, was finally drawing to an end! The adoption process was arduous, but we jumped through those home study hurdles as enthusiastically as one wounded couple can. We found a primary care doc and were deemed "medically fit" to be parents. We filled out the intense questionnaire.

"Will you take a child whose birth mom has been on drugs?"

"Will you take a child with special needs?"

On and on the probing questions went. We answered our social worker's absurd questions like, "How will you handle it if your child's race is different from your own? How will you respond to unwelcome questions and comments?" We played out one hypothetical scenario after another. We had to ask friends and family to fill out reference forms and mail them in about what kind of parents they thought we would be. It was intense, as you know.

Finally, the home study process was complete. It was then time for me to pour my heart and soul into our "profile." This scrapbook documented our lives. Our home, dreams, passions, puppy and extended family ... all bound together in one beautiful book!

Since I had quit my job when we thought we were having our first baby, I had plenty of time to make a ridiculously awesome profile book. I poured over fifty hours into it, praying over the pages and hoping so hard that the first birth mom who opened its pages would fall in love with us.

And she did, or so to speak. We'll call her "Jane." Jane picked us and since it would be an open adoption, we went to meet her. She was beautiful and kind. Her hair was brown and curly and her baby bump was enviably adorable. She was in a tumultuous relationship at the time and had two other boys she had chosen to raise. The baby in her womb was another boy.

Our meeting took place at the adoption agency and we sat (quite awkwardly) across the table from each other. Neither of us had ever met anyone in that context before. Kevin and I fumbled through our profile, my face red with fear and anticipation, and poured out our life stories. We introduced her to the people in the pictures. I tried (and failed) to shove my nerves back down where they belonged.

When we said goodbye that day, we exchanged hugs around her (our) baby belly and then Kevin and I walked quickly out to our car. My stress and excitement manifested itself as tears.

"It is really happening! We are going to be parents in a few short weeks!" Kevin took my face into his hands and put his forehead to mine. It was a sweet moment that I'll never forget.

Sigh.

A couple weeks later, at her request, we were to meet up again at the agency to talk about the birth plan. We arrived 15 minutes early, to show our punctuality, of course. (This was big for us, because we are the king and queen of tardiness.) I was a ball of nerves, yet again, and my nerves took on a life of their own when Jane never showed. We waited for a good hour.

Overall, our adoption anxiety rose a tad, but our social worker reassured us that everything was most likely fine. She said, "this kind of thing happens quite a bit. I'll let you know when I get ahold of her. It is probably just a transportation or communication issue."

So we continued to plan and wait for baby boy. We named him Carson and prayed for him (and for a smooth adoption) every waking moment.

My dream had always been to nurse my children so when I came across a book called "Nursing Your Adopted Baby" I got pretty pumped, pun intended. I heard from everybody and their mom how wonderful a "bonding experience" nursing was. I desperately wanted that, because ... who wouldn't? The book declared that almost everyone could nurse successfully without giving birth, so I set out to do just that.

Step one was: Get a breast pump and start pumping. Ceaselessly is what they meant to say when they said every two to three hours. So that's what I did. Whoa, let me tell you. It's weird as heck your first time, consider yourself warned. Finally, after a week or so of pumping, milk started to come. Just barely, but it was there. I was giddy when I saw that first drop.

Our social worker had reconnected with Jane and all systems were still a go. Her induction was set for just a few weeks later and our friends started planning our baby shower! It would be jungle themed to match the nursery. Carson's room renovation was coming right along and we didn't have a moment to lose ... or so we thought.

The weeks crawled by, and "our" baby grew, as did our excitement. On the morning before my baby shower, I headed out to the front porch to grab the freshly delivered boxes of baby paraphernalia I couldn't stop ordering. As I walked back inside, my phone rang. When you're adopting and your screen pops up with "Nancy the Social Worker," your heart inevitably skips about twenty three beats. I was hoping so deeply that our birth mama was in labor, but I feared the worst.

It was the latter. Jane had changed her mind, and her on-again-off-again-boyfriend's parents would be adopting the boy we had named and prayed for for weeks ... well, years.

It was crushing.

You and I, we put our dreams on the line in this world of adoption. We put our savings account on the line. And we subject ourselves to the pain of loss and sadness all over again. I'm so sorry that you've been hurt by a poorly-run country or a well-intentioned birth mommy. I'm crushed for you for the loss of your adopted child who you loved as your own, but whom the world doesn't understand as yours at all.

I thought our lives were over, but they weren't. We're still breathing, and you will rally too, in time. Our story didn't end there, and yours doesn't have to end with heartbreak either.

2 CORINTHIANS 4:8-9

THE MESSAGE

WE'VE BEEN SURROUNDED AND BATTERED BY TROUBLES, BUT WE'RE NOT DEMORALIZED; WE'RE NOT SURE WHAT TO DO, BUT WE KNOW THAT GOD KNOWS WHAT TO DO; WE'VE BEEN SPIRITUALLY TERRORIZED, BUT GOD HASN'T LEFT OUR SIDE; WE'VE BEEN THROWN DOWN, BUT WE HAVEN'T BROKEN.

I blogged about that "one little phone call." And would you

believe who saw it? Coleton's birth mommy. The one who was nineteen weeks pregnant and wanted to ask us if we could adopt her baby. The one who didn't know what to do because we were "adopting this other baby." The one God intended to see that blog. The one who knew deep down that Kevin and I were the ones who would raise her baby boy. She saw that blog and immediately reached out to me to see when we could meet. And the rest is history.

Have you ever had something happen that seemed devastating in the moment, but that ended up making sense later? Something you ended up being grateful for because without it you wouldn't be who you are now? Your failed adoption may very well become one of those moments.

I'm not saying "get over it." This hurts and you need to be where you are. But I am here to remind you not to doubt the masterpiece that's being created by your story, sweet girl.

God has a plan for your family, and for reasons we don't understand, it doesn't include raising the child you thought you would. But just maybe it includes raising a child you don't know yet, but who is already living inside the womb of a mommy who can't take care of him. Or in a city somewhere, yearning for a forever family.

Wait for the Lord. Be strong and let your heart take courage; wait for the Lord!

(PSALM 27:14)

"Life is tough my darling, but so
are you."

—Unknown

Leah's Story

Courage is knowing that it may not happen, but trying anyway.

—UNKNOWN

Hope.

Webster's Dictionary defines it as "wanting something to happen or be true; to think that it could happen or be true."

I can personally deem that definition as accurate. I have hoped for *years* I would have the honor and privilege to adopt a sweet child "grown in my heart, not under my heart." But that reality has never come to pass.

We started our adoption journey almost ten years ago. I have wanted to adopt my entire adult life. I felt the Bible was very clear about caring for the orphan. Having served in multiple orphanages around the world, I figured I could love one of those babies just as easily as I could a biological baby. So it was natural for adoption to be a topic of discussion from the moment my husband, Tony, and I started talking about marriage.

When we got married, we had every intention of expanding our family through adoption someday. That some day hit in 2007, when we had been married for seven years and had three biological children. We were ready; it was time to adopt! Little did we know, we would spend thousands of dollars, watch years go by, and never bring a brown-eyed child into our home.

I say "brown-eyed" because that was *our* expectation. My husband and I are both blue-eyed, as are each of our biological children are blue-eyed. We yearned for a brown-eyed babe to join our crew. Tony and I have been around the world serving, traveling, loving, and learning about God and His magnificent creation. Every trip, every country, every year … it always came back to the people.

We were designed to live in relationship with people and love like Jesus. He created such an amazing variety and we were thrilled to get to love on a small portion of His children. We longed to bring some of those babies into our home to show them Jesus as well as two humans could.

After paying for two home studies and multiple country changes, We started questioning whether we had heard God incorrectly. I didn't know if I could wait any longer or withstand any more changes. The world of international adoption was changing radically and dramatically. Sadly, it wasn't for the betterment of the abandoned children.

We were nearing the expiration of our home study (again)

but we decided we would continue to wait, hope, and pray. Then we got Malachi's referral. I dared to hope; not ask whether God was playing a trick on us but really *believe*, "Could this be the child we have been waiting for, for so long?!?

Sorrowfully, that wasn't our story. Through a flurry of paperwork, further examinations and evaluations, thousands more dollars, grants applied for, accepted and rejected … we waited.

We hoped. And then, we cried when our story came to an abrupt halt.

We were not going to be able to parent Malachi. We were never going to travel to his homeland, taste his food, dry his tears, or read him bedtime stories. We weren't going to get to kiss and hug him or laugh at his wobbly steps. A part of me died that summer. And with it, my hope.

But then … Jesus. How gently He scooped me up and held me close. How lovingly He let me cry and dried my tears. Our other children kept asking when were we going to get Malachi. When were we going to fly to pick him up?

We were tasked to point them towards our true hope, Jesus. Papa God is writing a different story for us, different than the one we first hoped.

It has been two years since that heartbreaking loss of Malachi's referral. We continue to pray and wait for God to move if

He wants to expand our family through adoption. We continue to stand convinced that the Bible is clear about our charge to love and care for the orphan.

> *Religion that God our Father accepts as pure and fault-less is this: to look after orphans and widows in their distress and to keep oneself from being polluted by the world.*
>
> (JAMES 1:27, NIV)

Orphan care isn't optional for Christians, it is a mandate. So we will do what we can to serve orphans in whatever capacity we can, whether it is through adoption or something else. We trust that God has a plan for our family.

I would love to have more children in my home, but whether or not it ever becomes a reality, I won't walk away from my faith. I won't place my hope in adopting children, because even a home bursting at the seams with amazing children will not bring ultimate fulfillment.

So I wait. I wait on my Jesus. I wait for his voice and I wait for his plan to unfold, whatever that means. If his plan includes us welcoming home a brown eyed baby, amazing. If it doesn't, I will trust then too.

My fulfillment rests in Jesus and the future he promises for me in heaven. Because of his death and resurrection, my sins have been forgiven and I can be in a right relationship with

God. *That is the gospel, the good news. So no offense, Mr. Webster, but I've changed the definition of hope to: Jesus.* He brings beauty from ashes. He lifts me up when I fall. And he is my beginning and my glorious end.

He is life. He is hope. He is enough.

CHAPTER 14

For the Survivors

I can't tell you how many people I've met who have spent time in this desert too, once upon a lonely time. Usually as they recount even snippits of their stories, a lump rises into their throats. Her tears put up a fight to stay inside. Because it hurt and it still hurts, even if the pain has dulled and they're not waiting anymore.

Maybe that is you. Whether a long time ago or just recently, you know what it's like to hurt and you never want to go back. Maybe thinking about that desert season still gives you a knot in your belly. You were probably afraid or angry. Likely you felt alone or misunderstood. Maybe you're one of the lucky few who remember good things about that time, like being particularly reliant on God or close to your spouse.

But somehow, you made it out alive, and you're a stronger woman for it. You and I and all the other women on this side of the desert are changed forever. We will never be the same. We'll never be able to revisit the innocence. Pregnancy announcements will always be different for us, not always bad. Just different. The experience of holding a newborn baby will always carry an extra weight. We will never say the "silly" things people said to us. (All the praise hands!)

We will forever be aware of the living, breathing little people who inhabit the world around us. Maybe there's a little girl or boy you think looks like your child would have. Or one with the name you used or would have used.

The children in our lives are treasured intimately; we can feel the weight of their miraculousness. Their features. Their voices. Their messy hair and baby teeth and chunky fingers. Their precious sleeping breaths. We recognize the fragility of it all.

We will forever love on and pray for bereaved mothers with compassion and sensitivity. Until the day we leave this world, we will long for heaven with intensity.

The desert changed us. It's bittersweet because we wish it were a place we had never walked, tasted, touched. But we are who we are today because of it.

I just want to remind you that your story is precious. And your pain is still valid, no matter how long it has been.

You are a survivor.

Questions for Further discussion

1. What were your predominant emotions during your time in the desert?

2. Do you think you still have some healing to work through? (Keep reading!)

3. Who knows your story?

4. Would it be healthy for you to spend time remembering your desert season and sharing hope of survival with those currently in it?

   - If yes, how will you start? (Start a blog, a support group, attend a support group, speaking engagements, journaling, church, something else?)

Alternatives are everywhere.

Testing.

Hormone Therapy.

Shots.

Surrogacy.

Childfree living.

Adoption.

Foster Care.

Chiropractic care.

IUI.

IVF.

Acupuncture.

Diet changes.

Essential Oils.

Natural Supplements.

Resting and waiting.

Prayerfully explore and pursue what you feel drawn to. Whatever you do, do "you" and don't let other's opinions color how you feel. **You know you better than anyone else.**

And whatever you do, don't ever stop taking those 10 second deep breaths.

"Sometimes the people around you won't understand your journey. They don't need to, it's not theirs."

—UNKNOWN

Katey's Story

Since I was a little girl, I wanted nothing other than to be a mom. I dreamed of being pregnant, dreamed up names, practiced with baby dolls and babysat any chance I got. I planned to get married and have kids soon after. I {like many women} took for granted that I would be able to get pregnant, carry a baby inside my body, give birth, and become a mother to a beautiful child.

When Kevin and I got married in June of 2010, we knew we wanted to start our family right away. He is older than I am, so he wanted to have more children quickly so he would get to experience as much of their lives as possible. And given my forever dream to be a mom, I was happy with that plan.

Turns out, God had a different plan in mind. Here's the medical deal, I don't ovulate. So we began the joyous fertility treatments. We did pills, we did internal ultrasounds, we did blood draws every other day, we did shots every single day for months, we did doctor's appointments weekly, we did hormones. In other words, we did "Katie is in the CRAZY BASEMENT." My poor husband.

Through all of the difficult months of fertility treatments, here is what I learned: if you had told me "do this for _____ months and you will get a baby," it would have been no biggy. The end would have justified the means. What I couldn't handle was not knowing when or if we would ever get a baby.

The only way I got through the shots, ultrasounds, doctors appointments, blood draws, pills, and on and on ... was with HOPE that it would lead me to my child. And when it didn't, not only was I cranky because I had gone through not-fun stuff, but also because we weren't closer to having a baby. So. not. fair.

After months of this nonsense, we felt like we were at a crossroad: we could go the IVF route or adopt. They're both very expensive, but IVF wasn't guaranteed. So we chose adoption.

That decision wasn't made without heartache, though. I have grieved and still sometimes find myself grieving the loss of creating a biological child. I am sad that I may never feel my baby kick while it's growing inside of me. I am devastated that my body cannot or will not do what I have dreamed of my entire life.

But at the end of the day, I knew that it was a step of faith that God wanted us to take. His plan was in motion, and I could feel it somehow. I had no idea why he was leading us the way he was, but we stepped off of the traditional path onto a new one.

I knew God had made families across oceans, across biology, across blood. And certainly God would create our family in his image. I knew no matter what happened, that when we welcomed a child into our family, I would be more thankful to experience parenthood than I ever would have been otherwise.

"I'm going to be someone's mom." I thought to myself, all the time. And that sentence gave me hope.

Two years later

I created a Facebook Community Page for our adoption journey and was blown away when friends started sharing it like crazy. It was only a matter of weeks before I was messaged by a distant friend who I had gone to college with. She said she was touched by our journey and wondered if we had considered surrogacy. I responded that it had crossed our minds briefly, but we hadn't done much research.

One day later, she messaged me back and said that although she didn't know much and had no experience, she knew in her heart that she was supposed to be a surrogate in her lifetime. She and her husband felt so blessed by their own children and felt like God had given her the ability to provide another family with a child. Then my eyes read the sentence that would change our lives forever:

"I know this may sound abrupt or out of the blue, but if

*you decide to go that route, I would LOVE to be consid-
ered to help you bring life into this world."*

Did you hear the angels singing right there? I did.

Kevin and I spent that night talking about the possibilities
and texting with Julie about some of the logistics. Kevin was
cautiously optimistic. I was over-the-moon excited (and a bit
overwhelmed.) As I look back, I feel like I should've felt
strange about this whole process, but I never did. It was a
sense of peace from day one. Bizarre.

Julie and I talked a bit more through text over the following couple days and she continued to reassure me of the
seriousness of her offer. This was for real. She was going to
bring a baby into this world that we would get to keep forever.
I pinched myself endlessly.

God is so good.

With the help of an attorney, a phenomenal doctor, this
angel of a woman, and our amazing families, our daughter
Kamdyn was placed skin-to-skin onto my chest almost exactly
a year later. I was finally a mommy.

**Our vibrant baby girl has two years under her belt al-
ready, and I don't take a day of her life for granted. I am
beyond grateful for the miracle of modern medicine and the
selfless gift of surrogacy that "Auntie JuJu" and her family
have given to us.**

Praise the Lord.

"When you go through deep waters, I will be with you."

(ISAIAH 43:2)

Lana's Story

"With a baby or without you are valuable, you are whole and you matter."

—THE AMATEUR NESTER

We tried for four years. Four agonizing years where everything and its mom revolved around making a baby. And then it happened! One sweet tiny baby started growing in my womb.

We were so relieved! This baby would be so worth the wait. Then, I lost him when I was eight weeks along. Just like that, the answer we felt like we had been praying and waiting for was stripped away.

After grieving that loss, we decided to try for one more year. If we didn't get pregnant in that year, we were going to stop. Stop striving. Stop timing. Stop all the madness and go on a trip to Switzerland. Why Switzerland? Because it sounded dreamy. On that trip into the snowy mountains, we would plan out what living child-free might look like.

When that twelve month mark rolled around, I could barely stand. I felt the heaviness of all the held breaths and lost years come crashing down. As we neared our trip, I basically lived "in mourning." I curled up into fetal position a lot, crying until I couldn't cry anymore.

These tears were different than the tears along the way, because this time we were done. My husband held me and we cried together over the loss of our dream to become parents. But we both felt a deeper hope rumbling under the surface, knowing that there was another way to live that didn't involve waiting. It didn't involve tests or probes or unknowns.

Under the pain, we agreed that there could be another way to live, "post infertility," that we could step into and perhaps even enjoy. Childfree living.

It was something I would have never considered earlier in the journey, but the losses and the waiting were slowly killing us.

We journeyed to a breathtaking cabin in Switzerland and cuddled up in front of a fireplace with a blank piece of paper. What now? What should we do with our lives? What *could* we do? The answers to these questions were much different than they were a month earlier.

We began a list. It was hard at first, and of course I cried a little bit here and there, but after working through some stuff, we started rolling. Some long lost excitement was awakened in us that we hadn't felt in years. We could still make a huge mark on the world, even if not through raising up our own children.

When we got home, we dove right in. I threw away my ovulation tests and prescription bottles. I took my reproduction doc out of my "favorites" in my iphone.

We were "Auntie Lana" and "Uncle J" to my sister's kids and we embraced that gig with our whole hearts. Those babes rock, and we are a pretty rockin auntie and uncle if I do say so myself.

We dove into the junior high ministry at our church and started loving on the kids, even and especially the chatty and annoying ones. It turns out those are the ones whose parents don't care too much to be involved in their lives. We have time to take them out for dinner, late night pie talks, and baseball games. We love them fiercely and we stand in the gap for them. These kids have blessed us immensely.

I hesitantly visited a the home of a friend who breeds dogs and fell in love with her puppies. ME! The girl who wouldn't have touched a dog with a ten foot pole as a kid. Blanchard and Macy became the first little ones we got to name, and we have taken up running with them. I can't believe it but I'm training for a marathon!

There are still days when I run through the park on the bike path and find myself gazing longingly at the moms smiling and chatting on the playground. Baby giggles have a tendency to tug at my heart, but the pain doesn't linger all day ... night ... month ... year. Pain comes but it goes pretty quickly too. **I have rediscovered my purpose.**

It's not the life I thought I would have at age 35, but I really do love my life. I don't dread waking up to rush to the bathroom and take another negative pregnancy test. I just wake up, take a long hot shower, and go to work doing a job I love. I went back to school and got my PhD so I could get out of the grade schools and teach at a local college. My husband and I travel abroad every summer with the students. My husband does freelance consulting work and we take weekends away to travel to different places around the US four times a year.

Our nieces, our pups, and our Junior High church kids are like our own, bringing us so much fulfillment and blessing. God has turned our mourning into something really beautiful, and I am so grateful for this opportunity to share my story. I hope that I can encourage someone who is fearing the decision of childfree living. **We are filled with joy, and truly believe we're living out the plan God has for us.**

"An infertile womb was not a wrench in God's plan, but a vessel to show his glory."

—Gloria Furman, Missional Motherhood

CHAPTER 15

Biblical

God has done crazy things. Things like speaking everything into existence from nothing. Things like embodying himself in a cloud, a burning bush, and a man named Jesus who was born to a virgin. Things like defeating armies of 135,000 with 300 people (Judges 7), closing the mouths of lions (Daniel 6). **Things like opening the wombs of women who were once infertile.**

In the Bible, you will find seven barren women who once lived in the desert of waiting, and seven barren women to whom God granted children.

These stories are astounding and inspiring, and I share them with you **not** so you can be like, "gee, thanks for telling us more stories of people who couldn't have a baby and then (TADA!) did," but so you can see how God moved in his Holy Word through women who have walked miles in your sand filled shoes.

Some of these women fasted and prayed and cried out to God. Some had resigned themselves to being infertile forever.

Most of them felt so sure their infertility was final that they laughed and stumbled back in <u>utter shock</u> when God gave them a baby.

The Bible calls itself *living and active, sharper than any two edged sword* ... (Hebrews 4:12) so I'll let God's word speak encouragement to you today in a way that my words can't.

Abraham and Sarah

Sarai was OLD. Not like AMA (Advanced Maternal Age, 35+) old. She and her husband, Abram, were 90 and 99 years old respectively! It was at that point in their wrinkly lives that God gave them the news that they would no longer be infertile. God announces to Abram that he would become the father of many nations, whose offspring would outnumber the stars in the sky.

Over the course of the narrative, God changes their names

to Abraham, which means "father of a multitude of nations," and Sarah, meaning "princess" from Sarai which meant "quarrelsome."

Bahaha! Exactly, they laughed! They were like, "God. Wait, you're joking right?! We're saggy, gray, and yeah, what do you mean we going to have more than a billion little people in our bloodline?!"

The Lord said to Abraham, "Why did Sarah laugh and say, 'Shall I indeed bear a child, now that I am old?' Is anything too hard for the Lord? At the appointed time I will return to you, about this time next year, and Sarah shall have a son."

(GENESIS 18:13-14)

That's exactly what happened. Sarah had a son and named him Isaac. ABRAHAM WAS 100 YEARS OLD WHEN HIS SON WAS BORN. One. Hundred. Years. Old. And Sarah said, *"God has made laughter for me; everyone who hears will laugh over me."* (Genesis 21:6).

Go ahead and laugh, but laugh because God has a sense of humor. And He moves in our lives even when we are tempted to just give up. He refines us in our waiting. He uses our trials to mold us into harder-better-faster-stronger people so we can point the glory right back where it belongs.

Isaac and Rebekah

Isaac was the son of Abraham and Sarah's union. Isaac was forty years old when he *prayed to the Lord for his wife, because she was barren. And the Lord granted his prayer, and Rebekah his wife conceived.* (Genesis 25:21)

Twinsies! And Clomid wasn't even around yet.

Jacob and Rachel

Jacob was one of the twins Isaac and Rebekah had. They had trouble conceiving too. In their story you'll notice overt jealousy, blame and marital strife caused by the infertility. (Ahh, yes, you aren't the only one.)

> *When Rachel saw that she bore Jacob no children, she envied her sister. She said to Jacob, "Give me children, or I shall die!" Jacob's anger was kindled against Rachel, and he said, "Am I in the place of God, who has withheld from you the fruit of the womb?"*
>
> (GENESIS 30:1)

After her husband had been given ten other sons by other women (can you imagine?), *God remembered Rachel, and God listened to her and opened her womb. She conceived and bore a son and said, "God has taken away my reproach." And she called his name Joseph, saying, "May the Lord add to me another son!"* (Genesis 30:22-24)

Indeed, she went on to have another son, but she lost her life in childbirth (as was common in that time).

Manoah and his wife

The angel of the Lord appeared to her (Manoah's wife) and said, "You are barren and childless, but you are going to become pregnant and give birth to a son. Now see to it that you drink no wine or other fermented drink and that you do not eat anything unclean. You will become pregnant and have a son whose head is never to be touched by a razor because the boy is to be a Nazirite, dedicated to God from the womb. He will take the lead in delivering Israel from the hands of the Philistines."

(JUDGES 13:3-5, NIV)

The woman gave birth to a boy and named him Samson. He grew and the Lord blessed him.

(JUDGES 13:24, NIV)

Samson grew up with supernatural strength given by God. We're talking killed-a-lion-with-his-bare-hands-strength. Slaying-an—army-with-a-donkey-jawbone-strong. Destroying-a-pagan-temple strong. Dang. Don't mess with Samson.

God could have tremendously huge plans for your future miracle children too, however he brings them into your life.

Elkanah and Hannah

The story of Hannah is my favorite infertility story in the Bible. Twice the scriptures say that God had closed her womb. But Hannah was a woman of God who cried out to Him in her lowest moments.

In her deep anguish Hannah prayed to the Lord, weeping bitterly.

(1 SAMUEL 1:10, NIV)

The priest, Eli thought she was drunk because of the intensity of her mourning. She told him that she was not drunk but just deeply troubled.

I was pouring out my soul to the Lord ... I have been praying here out of my great anguish and grief. Eli answered, "Go in peace, and may the God of Israel grant you what you have asked of him."

She said, "May your servant find favor in your eyes." Then she went her way and ate something, and her face was no longer downcast.

(1 SAMUEL 1:15-18, NIV)

Unlike most of these Bible women, Hannah believed it would happen even *before* it actually happened. I want to have faith like Hannah!

"Early the next morning they arose and worshiped before the Lord and then went back to their home at Ramah. Elkanah made love to his wife Hannah, and the Lord remembered her. So in the course of time Hannah became pregnant and gave birth to a son. She named him Samuel, saying, "Because I asked the Lord for him.""

(1 SAMUEL 1:19-20, NIV)

Hannah holds true to her word and devotes her son to the Lord. She brings him back to the temple when he is done nursing and says, *"I prayed for this child, and the Lord has granted me what I asked of him. So now I give him to the Lord. For his whole life he will be given over to the Lord."* And he *worshiped the Lord there.* (1 Samuel 1:27-28, NIV)

It's because of this account that we gave our firstborn son, Coleton, the middle name Samuel. He was the child we had waited, prayed, and cried out for that we got to finally welcome into our home. And we will devote him (and all of our children) to the Lord, just like Hannah did.

The Shunamite woman

"She has no son, and her husband is old."

Then Elisha said, "Call her." So he called her, and she stood in the doorway. "About this time next year," Elisha said, "you will hold a son in your arms."

"No, my lord!" she objected. "Please, man of God, don't mislead your servant!" (She was like NO! Don't lie to me! Don't get my hopes up!)

But the woman became pregnant, and the next year about that same time she gave birth to a son, just as Elisha had told her.

(2 KINGS 4:14B-17, NIV)

Elizabeth – Mother of John the Baptist and cousin of Mary

Meet Zechariah and Elizabeth.

… they were childless because Elizabeth was not able to conceive, and they were both very old."

(LUKE 1:7)

Then an angel appears to Zechariah and he freaks. But the angel says, "Do not be afraid, Zechariah; your prayer has been heard."
(Pretty much what we all long to hear.)

"Your wife Elizabeth will bear you a son, and you are to call him John. He will be a joy and delight to you, and many will rejoice because of his birth, for he will be great in the sight of the Lord."

(LUKE 1:13-15, NIV)

Elizabeth goes on to give birth to John the Baptist, whose ministry prepares the way for Jesus Christ.

That's a wrap

See what I mean? The Bible is full of mama wombs and arms that were once empty and ended up filled. You might not have an angel appear to you or a prophet speak over you, but God is the same yesterday, today, and forever. He is still a miracle worker and he is still in control, even when this broken world wreaks havoc in our lives.

Bonus Treasure: The Gospel

In the Old Testament, sacrifices had to continually be made to atone for sin. It was a flawed system, lending itself to constant striving and unrest. So God orchestrated a most beautiful rescue mission because he loved humankind and wanted to be in a right relationship with them again.

He sent his only son, Jesus, to be the once and for always payment for sin. Because of Jesus and his sacrifice on the cross, there would never again be a relational divide between God and mankind. Jesus' death and resurrection is why we can go directly to God with our prayers (and lives). He is the only one who can truly satisfy the deepest desires of our hearts.

Gospel means "good news." It's pretty earth-shatteringly phenomenal news that we don't have to survive all by our lonesomes in this hot mess of a world. We have a savior and his name is Jesus. We have a King for a daddy, an Abba, a perfect Father if we place our trust in him.

He is peace. He is life everlasting. He is the reason I can hope with assurance.

For God so loved the world that he gave his one and only son, that whoever believes in him shall not die but have eternal life.

(JOHN 3:16, NIV)

Questions for Further Discussion:

1. Did you know about all of those infertility accounts in the Bible? Which is your favorite?

2. Which Bible story do you best connect with? Why?

3. Do you desire to incorporate more time reading the Bible, God's word, into your life on a regular basis? How could you make this happen? (Appendix 2 has some additional Bible Study resources.)

4. Do you know Jesus Christ personally? If yes, how has this trial impacted your relationship with him? If no, do you feel like he is pursuing you? What will you do to respond?

"It is time."

—Rafiki, The Lion King

CHAPTER 16

Yours

YOUR
STORY
HOLDS
great
POWER

It's time for you to get your favorite pen out and give yourself the gift of telling **your** story. It may begin waaaaay back when you were a little girl or 1/10/20 years ago when you started "trying."

Your story may be only for you or it may be something you put out there for the world to see.

As you process your journey, you will start to uncover that power. As you write, you will understand more about yourself. And as you begin sharing it, you will see it bearing hope to people facing desert seasons of their own.

There is power in vulnerability. Go there.

If the sharing part freaks you out, don't think about it today. Just start by getting everything down on paper. Write through your physical, emotional, and spiritual experiences. Write down your hopes and prayers for the future, the ones you're afraid to murmur aloud because what if they don't come true?

In the coming weeks and months, revisit and scribble more down as you remember details or encounter new plot twists and turns.

This exercise will help you heal. Even if no one else ever reads what you write, you will look back someday and be glad you have an account of what happened. Because believe it or not, when you're out of the desert, you won't remember exactly what it felt like when you were in the middle of it.

I pray that this will help you, now *and* someday, see the hope God has birthed into and out of your life ... whether or not you ever bear children.

Here's a little writing guide to help you get going, but feel no pressure to stick to it (says the free spirit). Make it your own!

Beginning:

When did it start?

Where did these things take place?

When did I know something was wrong?

Where did we turn?

Who were the characters involved?

Where was I in my faith?

Middle:

What all did we try?

How did my heart hold up?

How did it affect my life?

How did it affect our marriage?

How did it affect my faith?

End:

Where am I now?

What do I hope my future looks like?

Where do I find joy in the meantime?

Which fun and healthy things do I want to do while I wait?

"It is not your love that sustains the marriage, but from now on, the marriage that sustains your love."

—DIETRICH BONHOEFFER

CHAPTER 17

Marriage

Marriage, what a wonderfully complex relationship. Two imperfect humans uniting together … the struggle is real!

If your marriage has been hit hard by the desert storms, let me pull you in close to whisper some truths over you.

Hold on for dear life, my beautiful darling. You're fighting the good fight. It is worth it. Every day. Every prayer. Every time you forgive. It's worth it more than you know. Your man needs you and you need him, and you can make it through this.

My friend, you are a fighter. You're fighting for children, but you are also fighting for your marriage! I don't want you to lose who you are as a couple are in the pursuit of having babies.

You guys will be in different places at different times along this desert road. You may not see eye to eye. Tension will surface. Miscommunications are inevitable. But I want to equip you with some practical ways you can fight for a healthy marriage, because you are a team. You need each other, and I don't want you to lose something you already have in the pursuit of something that isn't guaranteed.

Tip #1 Remember that he is a problem solver

He's going to get frustrated at times because he is wired to solve problems. He wants so badly to lift your burden, take your pain away, and get all the answers. He wishes he could sweep you up on a white horse and ride you straight out of the desert into a land flowing with milk and honey and babies. But it's Just. Not. That. Easy.

Not only can he not figure out an answer to getting a baby, but he wants to figure you out. But figuring out a hormonal, unpredictable woman can be quite scary and impossible, I imagine. We are complex and ever-changing.

*Men, if you ever wanted to know what a female mind

feels like, imagine a Chrome browser with 2,403 tabs open. All. The. Time.*

On Monday we might want to process (aka sulk) in silence but on Tuesday we might need to pour our hearts out. On Wednesday, we may want to go out, have fun, and pretend like everything is fine!

Honey bear sweet babyface husbands, I wish you could solve this too.

Tip #2: Acknowledge that your hubby is hurting too

He probably won't express his emotions the way you do, but it doesn't mean that he's not hurting. When you use hormones and circumstances as an excuse for mistreating him, you're kicking him when he's already down.

Of course hormones will cause some lash outs so out-of-body you can't even be held responsible for, but be aware of your tendencies and strive for humility. Asking for forgiveness is a beautiful (and stupidly hard) thing.

Your husband is a valuable person with feelings too! You must speak lovingly and communicate openly so he feels loved. Show him the same TLC you want to be shown.

Tip #3: Honor your differences

Decisions will pop up on this desert road that need to be made, but about which you will disagree wholeheartedly. Finding an agreement will be like trying not to eat seventeen candy bars on the day you find out you're not pregnant. Impossible. Compromises will have to ensue.

No matter how alike you are, there will be areas in which you will simply be different. Like, really different. Humans feel and think and perceive things differently because we weren't created to be the same. It doesn't mean you aren't compatible or that one of you is right and one is wrong.

I recently had an epiphany thanks to something so ridiculous you're going to laugh. Apple devices each come with a set of headphones. The older style of headphones were a perfect fit for me, but Kevin would complain that they hurt his ears. I would tell him to "get over it" and "man up, how bad could it be?!" (I'm embarrassed to admit that sometimes I can be a jerk face to that hottie. But there you have it.)

After a few years of free headphone nirvana, Apple switched things up and the exact opposite situation ensued. The new headphones fit Kevin like a glove and I cannot even touch them without my ears throbbing and writhing in pain. I'm not exaggerating. I would rather never wear headphones again than wear those new headphones. Which, as it turns out, is how he felt about the other ones. Because we are *different*.

Neither of us is wrong. We're just different. (Now props where props are due, Kevin didn't tell me to get over it. He was sweet and kind and ordered me the old style because I lose everything and he is saintly like that.)

So often I fail to appreciate our differences. Instead, I want him to be the same as me. Think like me. Eat like me. Shop like me. Vote like me. Cry like me. (When I write it out, I recognize the sheer ridiculousness of it; I really do.)

When we were waiting for a child, I wanted him to be on the same wavelength and timeline as me. When we didn't agree, I thought he should defer to me since it was my body going through the pregnancies and losses. And although he was sensitive to that (and should have been), treating his opinion as less important was wrong. Our men's feelings and opinions matter too. They matter so very much. And when I stop to think about it, I'm grateful my man *isn't* as emotional or spaghetti-brained as I am. (We would be a blazing mess!)

I'm thankful to have a partner, whether or not it is always easy. Marriage is hard and good. And all good things are worth fighting for.

Tip #4: Investing in your marriage is just as important as investing in having children

Start with a date night. Y'all need to celebrate who you are as a couple, and how far you've come. Send him a sweet little invitation. Set a reservation. Throw on that sexy little number hanging in the back of your closet. Do up that hair. Do what you need to do to feel attractive again!

Make it a special night of reconnection. Flirt with your man! Kiss him a little longer. Hold his gaze like you haven't done in months. Woo him like you're dating again. Tell him your favorite things about him. Pep talk your man like never before (men eat that stuff up)! Give him a speech about how much he means to you and how you're committed to your marriage, come whatever the heck may.

Talk about stuff you both love. Make up "would you rathers." Laugh together! Find a concert or an experience to share. Discover new places where you won't see kids! Reminisce about how much you have both changed for the better since the night you first met. Toast to all that you've survived!

Rekindle the romance. I'm not *just* talking about sex, but doing that won't hurt either. *Not babymaking sex.* **Making love.** It might take all your energy to be present and get "in the mood," but I believe in you. You can get there. Light some candles. Turn on some music. Give each other massages. Do whatever you used to do.

Some high quality date nights and some good old fashioned love making can work wonders.

I mentioned earlier that professional marriage counseling is something we also invested in. We did it reluctantly at first but we pretty much knew our communication rut wasn't going away without some assistance. My emotions were too jumbled to voice clearly on my own. Quickly, counseling became something we recommended to anyone and everyone. Lots of churches offer it as a free service too, if moolah is what's holding you back.

Don't be afraid to invest in and fall back in love with the man you spoke those vows to. You need each other more than ever. **There isn't an investment more valuable.**

Tip #5: Become a grace giver

He's going to mess up. You're going to mess up. Grace has to be present for a marriage to survive and thrive.

And when he screws up? Well, you are going to love him anyway. Because he's human and humans aren't perfect. You're going to need to become a grace giver.

Grace is giving someone something even and especially when they don't deserve it. Kinda like how Jesus loved and died for us while we were still sinners. (Romans 5:8). He's the world's best grace giver.

Also, a grace giver is way more attractive than a bitter old lady.

Tip #6: Stop expecting him to read your mind

How is your handsome hunk supposed to love you well without knowing what you want and need? He can't read your mind (thank goodness)! He couldn't then, he can't now, nor will he ever be able to. Bless his heart. You have to communicate your wants, needs, and feelings.

At the same time, you need to be mindful of not talking his ear off. (I am the guiltiest among us, so don't think I'm casting the first stone. Sometimes Kev and I literally set a timer for our convos so I don't blubber and blab for an amount of time that no human could realistically stay engaged.)

Tip #7: Give passive aggressiveness the chopping block

I know, I know. Easier said than done. But it hurts both of you. It breeds bitterness. Weeding this one out is difficult, but start by setting up a conversation to talk about your feelings. Pray it up. Prepare (maybe on paper) what you need to share from your heart about how you're feeling and what you desire from him. This convo will provide a safe space to be open and honest, rather than skirting around the issue or "dropping hints." Men just aren't subtle creatures. They need us to spell it out!

Especially in a tense situation like grief, being passive aggressive will only frustrate and blur communication. Our marriage is much easier when we are gentle, humble, and **direct** about what we want and need.

Tip #8: Write him notes and letters

Writing can help you sort out your feelings and thoughts, and it can be infinitely more digestible for him because it removes the "female emotions" that get him all flustered. Your words will give him insight into how he can best support you through this time. As a bonus, you can encourage and express your support for him too.

One of my many letters to my husband in the midst of our darkness looked like this:

Dear Kev,

I desperately want to hold a little baby and see a little "YOU" looking back up at me. I so wish the day would hurry up and get here ... the day when I hear those cutie little voices shrieking "daddy!!!!" when you walk through the door after work. I can't wait to hear their giggles as you wrestle and tickle fight on the living room floor. **You will make such an amazing daddy.**

You already make an amazing husband. Thank

you for being the ever-steady-you and for holding my hand through this crazy last three and a half years. As terrifying and as hard as this road has been, I know that it would be exponentially harder without you to lean on.

You've been patient with my hormonal, hissy-fitty rants, my angry moments and my tears that sometimes can't be stopped. I'm sure when you said "I do" you had no idea how messy and confusing (and I'm sure terrifying) a woman's emotions could be ... or how many of your white shirts I would stain with mascara. Yet you have stuck by my side day after difficult day and words cannot express how grateful I am.

I'm sorry for the times that I have hurt your feelings and pushed you away. I struggle with guilt that "I can't give you babies." I know how much you want them, and I know you don't blame me ... but I am really struggling with that.

Although I wouldn't wish this trial on anyone, I know that God in his sovereignty has chosen this for us to walk through. I know that He will provide the strength we need, and the strength to grow closer to Him and each other through it.

I'm working on "being content whatever the circumstances" (Phil 4:11) but we both know how much easier said than done that is. I know we will come out stronger on the other side, but since we're still in the midst of it, I want to share some ideas of ways to help me, especially on the days when I'm a hot mess:

- Simply sit with me. Rub my back or just listen.
- Don't try to stifle my emotions. Bring me the Kleenex and let me cry. You're pretty good at this. (I have your mom to thank for teaching you in advance how emotional women can be.)
- Talk to me about how you're doing and what God is teaching you.
- I know you're wired to "fix things" (and you're good at it!) but it's more helpful for me when you don't try to solve it-the physical limits or the emotional turmoil.
- Pray for me. The times that you've prayed over me are the times I feel the closest to God. I feel like he is so tangibly present. I know you're also praying for me even when we're not together, and I appreciate it more than you know.

I don't want our infertility/miscarriages to rob us of the joy that the marriage bed was created to be. I'm praying that God will restore the joy and passion that at times we feel like we've been stripped of.

Thank you for being vulnerable and showing me your weaknesses on this journey. I am so glad we're in this together.

Even if our battle with infertility is lifelong, I want you to know that no matter what ... no matter how many times I could have done it over ... I would choose you to be my husband every time. I would go through all of this again in a heartbeat to be with you. We will get through this.

I love you,

Livvie

Your note will look different, but it will be so good. Go forth and do these things, my lovelies! You will look back in thirty years and be so glad you didn't give up.

Where you go I will go and where you stay I will stay ...

(RUTH 1:16 NIV)

Questions For Further Discussion:

1. How is your marriage holding up?
2. How is your husband handling the waiting?
3. Has this trial brought you closer together or pushed you further apart?
4. Could you benefit from professional marriage counseling?
5. Have you written a letter to your husband lately? If no, do it!

"Community exists when we're willing to get dirty, do ugly and stay in the mess."

—Whenmercyfoundme.com

CHAPTER 18

Community

Have you ever been a part of a community? A sports team? A play or musical? A healthy church? Anything bigger and better than yourself?

Community, done well, can be powerful beyond measure. But for you to get to that deeper level, you have to let the walls come down.

As much as I wish this book could personify itself and magically transport me to your living room (in the least creepy way possible), no book can replace a real friend. A human can put her hand on your back, pray for you, weep with you. A sister can hand you tissues. A brother can bear hug you like there's no tomorrow. They can listen as you process, grieve, change, and discover hope.

This vulnerability, this bond that forms with your closest circle is a gift.

Vulnerability is a tangible treasure in a world where people masquerade around with their real selves hidden. **When people are real and raw, it is powerful and precious.**

By sharing yourself and your story with people, you are taking a risk. It's terrifying, but by doing it you are opening a door to something beautiful. Imagine the feeling Dorothy had when she walked into the land of Oz, not even realizing she had been living in black and white.

Community is a colorful new world of encouragement, truth, friendship, and unconditional love.

Your story is precious and meant to be shared. A trusted friend or circle of them is a safe place to start. Have you never ever told people about the madness that is your life right now? Start there. Keep it vague if that helps. Over time, you'll taste and see how good it feels.

As people earn your trust, you'll unearth the courage to share it again. And again. You'll discover the strength to speak aloud about the deepest, darkest, most painful details. And your true friends will not only not abandon you, they'll shelter you with love. And they'll generously dole out hope for you to borrow until you can find and bear your own again. That's real community.

The more you share your story, the more inspiration you'll be able to pour into the world. Your friends will reciprocate vulnerability, too. Their stuff will be different than yours, but as you exchange your chaos back and forth, you'll experience the sacred. The holy, mask-free sharing of your whole hearts and lives. I'm talking all the chaos. All the madness. The highest tippie mountain tops and the deepest, widest valleys.

When you're a weepy mess she'll provide you with words of strength and encouragement. She'll start quoting pinterest quotes at you like "it's going to be okay in the end. If it's not okay, it's not the end." She will say cliches like "you're not alone and I'm here for you no matter what" and you'll feel the truth of them down to your bones. And when you walk away from her house, swollen face and all, you'll wonder why you ever considered not sharing it.

Then someday, you'll be the one handing over the tissues and chocolate. This is real friendship and community, the way it was meant to be.

And guess what? The sad, scary, painful chapter of your story that's being written right now will be the one that will speak to that girl sitting on your couch in a heap in a couple years. The one who will be exactly where you are right now.

She will need herself a Sherpa who can guide her to the living water in the desert and remind her that she will make it out alive, just like you did.

Where can you even start to find these people?

- Support Group
- Small group (Churches usually offer lots of options)
- Church
- Neighbors
- Sisters and sisterfriends
- Relatives
- Online (A screen isn't the warmest fuzziest friend or my first recommendation but there are some incredible support groups on Facebook and around the web that can be less intimidating for a start!)

Ask God to show you who you can open up to. Pray that you will find your "tribe." Pray for opportunities to help others who are hurting like you. Sometimes when God answers my prayers, I get all surprised as if I hadn't just asked him for that very thing. Then I put my palm to my forehead and thank Him for His goodness even amidst my lack of faith. He hears our prayers.

The prayer of a righteous person has great power as it is working.

(JAMES 5:16B ESV)

Because he bends down to listen, I will pray as long as I have breath.

(PSALM 116:2 NLT)

Questions for Further Discussion

1. **List one person or place you will seek out and open up to this week.**

2. **You can do this! When and how will you reach out to them?**

* Tip: Lend your book to your friends to read Appendix 1: For Friends and Family. It will give them some ideas on how to be helpful to you in this season. Write them little notes ... highlight ... star your favorite parts. They can also download a free copy of the chapter at livryan.com/dear friends and family.

"The word of God is a gushing river providing rich sustenance in barren lands."

—LIV RYAN

CHAPTER 19

Elpiz

One of my favorite words is Elpis (pronounced: el-peez). It's a little Greek word that packs a huge punch. My favorite part of its definition is "joyful and confident expectation of eternal salvation, on hope, in hope, having hope." Elpis-type-hope offers promise that when we die, heaven will be there with lasting fulfillment.

I love elpis because everything in this world has flaky returns. Hopes are dashed every single gosh darn day. Lives are torn apart. Hearts are broken. But elpis means there is hope that surpasses physical circumstances.

It is hope that heaven exists, and that it's a place where tears are no more.

No amount of words I could write will guarantee you children. Nothing I could say will take away your pain. But I can spark hope anew in you because heaven can be counted on. Always and forever. It was that and only that, the promise of eventual glory, that kept me from laying down in the sand and saying "I quit" in so many moments along the way.

there is always hope

My girl, as your desert drags on and your nights fall dark and scary, I extend to you some words of hope and comfort from the Bible. You can come back to them (or any of the treasures scattered throughout this book) when you're hurting or need some extra sustenance. You can write them on your mirrors. You can stash them in your pockets. You can do whatever you want with them.

- *Your word is a lamp to my feet and a light to my path.* (Psalm 119:105)

- *This hope we have as an anchor of the soul, a hope both sure and steadfast and one which enters within the veil ...* (Hebrews 6:19, NASB)

- *"Is anything too hard for the Lord?"* (Genesis 18:14)

- *"The LORD is my portion," says my soul, "therefore I will hope in him."* (Lamentations 3:24)

- *God is not man, that he should lie, or a son of man, that he should change his mind. Has he said, and will he not do it? Or has he spoken, and will he not fulfill it?* (Numbers 23:19)

- *You are my hiding place and my shield; I hope in your*

word. (Psalm 119:114)

❖ *Let your unfailing love surround us, Lord, for our hope is in you alone.* (Psalm 33:22, NLT)

❖ *The Lord is near to the brokenhearted and saves the crushed in spirit.* (Psalm 34:18)

❖ *And my God will supply every need of yours according to his riches in glory in Christ Jesus.* (Phil 4:19)

❖ *May the God of hope fill you with all joy and peace as you trust in him, so that you may overflow with hope by the power of the Holy Spirit.* (Romans 15:13)

❖ *For in this hope we were saved. Now hope that is seen is not hope. For who hopes for what he sees? But if we hope for what we do not see, we wait for it with patience.* (Romans 8:24-25)

❖ *Be strong, and let your heart take courage, all you who wait for the Lord!* (Psalm 31:24)

❖ *For you formed my inward parts; you knitted me together in my mother's womb. I praise you, for I am fearfully and wonderfully made. Wonderful are your works; my soul knows it very well.* (Psalm 139:13-14)

❖ *The sacrifices of God are a broken spirit; a broken and contrite heart, O God, you will not despise."* (Psalm 51:17)

❖ *Jesus said to him, "I am the way, and the truth, and the life.* (John 14:6a)

❖ *God is our refuge and strength, a very present help in trouble. Therefore we will not fear, though the earth should change and though the mountains slip into the heart of the sea; though its waters roar and foam, though the mountains quake at its swelling pride. Selah. The LORD of hosts is with us; the God of Jacob is our stronghold. Selah."* (Psalm 46:1b-3, 7)

❖ *For everything that was written in the past was written to teach us, so that through the endurance taught in the Scriptures and the encouragement they provide we might have hope.* (Romans 15:4, NIV)

❖ *Therefore, since we have been justified through faith, we have peace with God through our Lord Jesus Christ, through whom we have gained access by faith into this grace in which we now stand. And we boast in the hope of the glory of God. Not only so, but we also glory in our sufferings, because we know that suffering produces perseverance; perseverance, character; and character, hope. And hope does not put us to shame, because God's love has been poured out into our hearts through the Holy Spirit, who has been given to us.* (Romans 5:1-5)

❖ *So we fix our eyes not on what is seen, but on what is unseen. For what is seen is temporary, but what is unseen is eternal.* (2 Corinthians 4:18, NIV)

❖ *Always be joyful. Never stop praying. Be thankful in all circumstances, for this is God's will for you who belong to Christ Jesus.* (1 Thessalonians 5:16-18, NLT)

❖ *Jesus said to her, "Everyone who drinks of this water will be thirsty again, but whoever drinks of the water that I will give him will never be thirsty again. The water that I will give him will become in him a spring of water welling up to eternal life." (John 4:13-14)*

❖ *Fear not, for I am with you; be not dismayed, for I am your God; I will strengthen you, I will help you, I will uphold you with my righteous right hand. (Isaiah 41:10)*

❖ *I keep my eyes always on the LORD. With him at my right hand, I will not be shaken. (Psalm 16:8, NIV)*

❖ *He alone is my rock and my salvation, my fortress where I will not be shaken. (Psalm 62:6, NLT)*

❖ *Casting the whole of your care [all your anxieties, all your worries, all your concerns, once and for all] on Him, for He cares for you affectionately and cares about you watchfully. (1 Peter 5:7, Amplified)*

❖ *The Lord is good, a Strength and Stronghold in the day of trouble; He knows (recognizes, has knowledge of, and understands) those who take refuge and trust in Him."* (Nahum 1:7, Amplified)

❖ *But now, Lord, what do I look for? My hope is in you.* (Psalm 39:7, NIV)

❖ *He brought me out into a spacious place; he rescued me*

because he delighted in me. (Psalm 18:19, NIV)

❖ *Jesus looked at them and said, "With man this is impossible, but with God all things are possible."* (Matthew 19:26)

❖ *Rejoice in hope, be patient in tribulation, be constant in prayer.* (Romans 12:12)

❖ *And I heard a loud voice from the throne saying, "Behold, the dwelling place of God is with man. He will dwell with them, and they will be his people, and God himself will be with them as their God. He will wipe away every tear from their eyes, and death shall be no more, neither shall there be mourning, nor crying, nor pain anymore, for the former things have passed away."* (Revelation 21:3-4)

Questions for Further Discussion:

1. Which scriptures spoke to you?
2. Which are hard for you to believe or understand?

Ideas for further study:

- Journal your observations and feelings about verses or passages of scripture.
- Memorize them.
- Read them aloud.
- Study their context and origin.

"You have turned for me my mourning
into dancing; you have loosed my
sackcloth and clothed me
with gladness"

(PSALM 30:11)

CHAPTER 20

Dancing

This desert season can't and won't hold you hostage forever. But while you're here, you might as well spend some time at the oasis refilling your canteen and letting go of the unbearable burdens. Go ahead and put your arm around that girl over there who desperately needs to know she isn't alone. Remind one another that God hasn't forgotten about you.

Remember that whichever way your path from the desert leads you, you're the beautiful protagonist we're all cheering for. You are the hero placing one boot in front of the other. And you're dang brave.

So slip on some sunglasses and hold your beautiful head high. Someday, this desert of waiting will deliver you into a new place. A spacious place filled with freedom and life, dancing and gladness, wine and celebrating, milk and honey. You'll shake the sand out of your boots, slip into some dancing heels, and everyone will gather around to hear your story of survival.

It might be in this lifetime, and it might be on the other side of eternity. But it'll be a darn good dance party. And we'll relish it all the more because of where we've been.

So I'm sending you snuggles and snacks to get you through today, hope enough for tomorrow, and prayers for the journey ahead.

Hang in there, sweet sister, just a little ways longer. Because this isn't the end. Whether or not you ever bear children, you can still bear hope.

I'd love to pray over you as we bear hug and part:

Lord, I lift my sister up to you. Draw her in close. Captivate her. Give her your water that satisfies. Help her embrace your words of hope. I pray that she would find freedom even in the wait and trust you passionately all the while. I pray that you would show her glimpses, if not fully, how you are in control and how it will all work together for good, both earth-side and eternally. Wrap your arms around her and hold her close, especially in her most vulnerable and painful moments. When she is tempted to get angry or fearful about the future, help her stand in faith and trust your way out. Help her feel you carrying her when she is too weak. Help her feel your presence always. Thank you for being a perfect Father. Last but not least, I ask boldly that you would settle her in her home as the happy mother of children as she delights herself in you.

In Jesus' name,
Amen.

For Friends and Family

"You have been my friend," replied Charlotte. "That in itself is a tremendous thing."

—EB WHITE, CHARLOTTE'S WEB

How can you be the awesome friend that your friend can't live without as she walks through the darkness of waiting for a child? I wish there were a perfect answer.

But the fact that you're reading this means that you care, and that is a fabulous place to start. It means more to your friend than she could ever put into words. Helping someone grieve is an art, not a science. But there *are* some things you can do to provide support.

Be available

Your hurting friend definitely needs you more than ever. Bring her favorite foods over. Do a coffee or smoothie drive by. Invite her out for a walks or runs or late night movies. She might need to talk about stuff or she may just want to talk about anything and everything other than babies. She doesn't want you to stay away just because she isn't herself. So find a way to be there for her, physically. Hold her if she needs a shoulder to sob on. Put your hand on her back. Hug her like you mean it. Snuggles provide physical sustenance and strength.

To say or not to say

What she needs most is encouragement and friendship, not advice or promises you can't deliver on.

"It will happen ..." is an example of something no one can be sure about. If you want to read a more comprehensive (and silly) list of things to keep a 10-foot pole away from, read chapter five.

Some helpful things you can say if her infertility or loss comes up:

o   "I'm sorry. That must be so hard. How are you handling everything?"

o   "Do you want to talk about it?"

o Could I bring over dinner sometime? (Ask for specifics rather than offering general help if she needs it.)

o I bought you this bracelet/necklace/ornament to symbolize your courage/strength/patience in this journey. Encourage her!

If you are pregnant

If she's a close friend, avoiding her will only cause her more pain. She needs her "people" more than ever before, whether or not you're pregnant or have a brood of kids. You can be sensitive to her by asking how she's doing and understanding if she doesn't want to talk a ton about yours.

A considerate way to announce your pregnancy to her is to go on a walk with her so she doesn't have to look you in the eye as you break the news, but you are still able to tell her in person. If you know it will be too hard for her, send her a handwritten note or a personal email before you make an announcement at large.

Validate how hard you know it will be to her, even though you know she's happy for you. If she cries, it's not because she is upset with you. It's because she wishes she could reciprocate the announcement. Embrace her tears! If you can help it, don't get awkward. Just be yourself. Hand over some tissues and be comfortable with silence.

A special way to love your friend is to be mindful of voicing your pregnancy woes. Of course you'll have them but don't complain about your pregnancy around her! She would practically sell her soul to be pregnant and feel those aches and pains in your place. She would give up wine and sushi and caffeine in a heartbeat to hear her own little one's heartbeat. She can't sympathize the way she normally would.

Pray for her and encourage her

If you are the praying type, please please please pray for her! Pray that she will have a healthy baby soon! Pray for her heart. Pray that she will embrace God's plan and timing for her life. Prayer is powerful, and we could all use more of it in our lives. Let her know you're supporting her in this way!

Scripture is **full** of promises and encouragement. When I was struggling, I remember receiving a specific card in the mail that was full of handwritten scriptures. These words pierced my heart (like the Bible usually does) and I wept grateful tears as I read it.

Point her to the words in the Bible when she feels hopeless *and when she seems good.* I've pointed out some hope-filled verses throughout this book too (especially in Chapter 19, Elpis).

Stick around and be patient

Please don't give up on her! This journey can be extremely long and drawn out. We're talking years upon years upon years. The intensity and weight of her wait may become burdensome for you too, but you can be such a light in her life. Keep praying. Keep asking how she is doing. Keep loving. Keep on, friend. Your friendship and your sacrifices are making eternal ripples.

Thank you for caring. You are amazeballs and your crown in heaven is getting sparkly. Not to mention, I know she'll return the favor someday.

APPENDIX II

Resources

Support Groups

- There isn't a one-stop shop as far as a support group database goes (especially if you live in a smaller city). But if you search online for "(Faith based) support groups for infertility/child loss in <u>your city</u>," you might be able to find one! If you can't find one close, consider driving to the next big city. *It's that worth it.*

- Online Support Groups are everywhere on Facebook. I recommend the Hope Mommies Support group for loss and Sarah's Laughter and Waiting for Baby Bird for infertility. There are smaller ones you can find or create within those.

- If you have a fire in your belly to connect with and love on others, consider starting a support group in your area!

- Sarah's Laughter hosts an annual conference full of resources and support. I would highly recommend it!

- Find a Resolve infertility support group at: resolve.org/support/support-groups.html

Counselors

Some churches offer Biblical counseling which can be a great option. If you would rather find a licensed counselor, a personal recommendation is ideal. Your friends, OB, RE, or pastors might have suggestions. Or search online for counselors in your area. Call around and ask questions like:

- What kind of experience do you have with infertility/pregnancy loss/child loss counseling?
- What is your philosophy of counseling?
- Do you provide faith-based support?
- What should I expect when I come?
- How much does a session cost? What types of insurance/payment plans do you accept?
- Whatever else you want to know!

It may take a few phone calls or even meeting with a couple different counselors before you find one that you really connect with. It's worth the hunt.

Online Support

www.resolve.org

www.ihr.com/infertility

www.Stirrup-queens.com

www.Waitingforbabybird.com

www.Sarahs-laughter.com

(They have a database of some support groups, but don't give up if your area isn't listed)

www.hopemommies.org

(For Loss: they host an annual retreat and have a phenomenal online support community)

Books

Every Bitter Thing is Sweet by Sara Hagerty

31 Days of Prayer During Infertility by Lisa Newton

Waiting for God to Fill the Cradle: One Month Devotional For Couples by Eric and April Motl

Anchored in Hope: Devotionals for Infertility by Ali Forrest

The Infertility Companion: Hope and Help for Couples Facing Infertility (Christian Medical Association) by Sandra. L Glahn and William R Cutrer

When Empty Arms Become a Heavy Burden by Sandra Glahn & William Cutrer, MD

Hope for Today, Promises for Tomorrow by Teske Drake

Choosing to See: A Journey of Struggle and Hope by Mary Beth Chapman and Ellen Vaughn

Hannah's Hope: Seeking God's Heart in the Midst of Infertility,

Miscarriage, and Adoption Loss by Jennifer Sakke

Plus or Minus: Keeping Your Life, Faith, and Love Together Through Infertility by Matt and Cheri Appling

Bittersweet by Shauna Niequist

Hearing Jesus Speak Into Your Sorrow by Nancy Guthrie

Holding On to Hope: A Pathway through Suffering to the Heart of God by Nancy Guthrie

Bible Study Resources

www.shereadstruth.com

www.ifequip.com

www.walkintheword.com

www.lproof.org

More Awesome Ministries and Resources

www.bethany.org

www.drewsfaithfulfeet.com

www.mamiespoppyplates.com

www.nofoottoosmall.org

APPENDIX III

Music

Liv's Bearing Hope Playlist on Spotify:

http://tinyurl.com/zq2dqbt

Albums for Healing:

Beauty Will Rise by Steven Curtis Chapman

As Sure as the Sun by Ellie Holcomb

You Make me Brave: Bethel Music

Freedom: Michael W. Smith

Church Songs: Vertical Church Band

APPENDIX IV

Adoption

"A child born to another woman calls me mommy. The magnitude of that tragedy and the depth of that privilege are not lost on me."

—JODY LANDERS

Adoption brings parents into the lives of orphans and children into the arms of the childless. It can be breathtakingly beautiful. I could share adoption stories all night long that would make your heart swell up like the Grinch's, but making the decision to venture into the world of adoption is personal and multifaceted.

Does it excite you? Freak you out? Where are you at with it?

Maybe you don't feel called to adopt or don't want to go there. It's all good! Skip right along, m'darling.

Were we nervous about adoption? HECK TO THE YES. Just like in every other huge life decision, fear reared its nasty head. But we chose to step out in faith anyway. We felt a pull, a nudge in our hearts that we couldn't shake.

Some questions to consider and discuss with your

spouse regarding adoption:

- o **Are you both open to it? Now? Down the road?**
- o **International or Domestic? Foster care? Foster to adopt?**
- o **Do you know anyone who has adopted who might share their story with us?**
- o **Are there local adoption agencies where you live?**
- o **Which other agencies would you consider?**
- o **What are the financial ramifications? Are you open to raising or saving the money needed to cover the adoption?**

Write down any and all of your questions. Social workers, adoption attorneys, and adoptive families will be happy to answer what they can.

The internet is a an exploding library stacked with blogs and websites on the topic. We're talking thousands if not millions!

As you consider all the questions and seek out more info, let this truth tumble around your brain: **Adopted children are your children.** God simply chose a different method of placing them into your family. If a dog or cat can become a legit part of your family, don't you think a human can too? Kevin and I would give up our lives for any of our children in a split second.

"If the standard route for creating a family had worked for me, I wouldn't have met this child. I needed to know her. I needed to be her mother. She is, in every way, my daughter."

—NIA VARDALOS, ACTRESS, SCREENWRITER AND AUTHOR OF
INSTANT MOM

Can adoption present unique obstacles in parenting? Absolutely! But every single child, whether biological or adopted, brings with him or her a set of challenges.

I'm beyond grateful that I got to experience firsthand what it looks like for a child to be *grafted in.*

With adoption, there might and probably will be more waiting. Think of yourself as an "expert" in waiting. An expert is defined as someone with 10,000 hours or more of practice in a particular area.

There may be a financial hurdle, but don't get ahead of yourself with fear. The internet is your friend when it comes to fundraising, my darling. You can find a bagillion ideas on how to raise money. There has been an adoption tax credit for years that helps cover a huge chunk of expenses. There are companies galore that help their employees with adoption assistance.

If you feel led toward adoption, this is the best piece of advice I can pass on:

"Feel the fear and do it anyway."

—SUSAN JEFFERS

One big fundraiser we did was a "Family Fun and Fitness Morning" with an entry fee that included Zumba, Holy Yoga and yummy bagels and coffee donated by local businesses. We raised over $1000 that morning!

We sold T-shirts. We save-save-saved. And then there were days when we opened our mailbox and found letters and donations from friends that brought us to our knees.

Countless adoptive families have raised tens of thousands of dollars to bring their children home, so don't let finances be a road block for you before you even consider the journey.

When I think about how many adopted kids would not have forever families had infertility not been a part of their story somehow, I am moved to tears. **God has a plan for your waiting. Maybe it's to adopt, and maybe it's not … but there is a plan.**

It doesn't matter what order or fashion they come into our families, ours are ours and yours are yours and it's *all* **crazy and cool (and challenging) and utterly breathtaking.**

Childfree Living

Living childfree involves making a decision to stop pursuing children, whether biologically or through any other means. There's a point on some women's journeys where enough is enough. Stepping away from the pursuit of children after years of wanting them takes so much courage, and the women from my support group who have done this are some of the bravest I know. For them, the thought of starting any other process that might result in children just felt like too much ... "Not gonna happen" they finally said.

Maybe that's you. You are ready to stop yearning. Waiting. Trying. Agonizing.

You can. You will know when or if it is time to embrace living childfree, or accept the child/children that you have as enough. This decision can have have ramifications for a marriage that need to be counseled through, especially when one person is "done" and the other isn't. We all know it's not as easy as 1-2-3, but making a decision to live childfree can be incredibly freeing.

It can hold so much hope and promise as you're able to finally make plans and dive into things you have been waiting on for years.

Maybe it involves:
- Traveling
- Caring for children who aren't yours
- Respite care for special needs families
- Ministry
- A new career
- Animals

Go forth, be an adventurer! And no matter what, bear hope.

Made in the USA
San Bernardino, CA
30 July 2016